The Authority of Service and Love

A Recovery of Meaning

The Authority of Service and Love

A Recovery of Meaning

Roger Payne

CHRISTIAN
ALTERNATIVE

Winchester, UK
Washington, USA

First published by Christian Alternative Books, 2017
Christian Alternative Books is an imprint of John Hunt Publishing Ltd.,
Laurel House, Station Approach,
Alresford, Hants, SO24 9JH, UK
office1@jhpbooks.net
www.johnhuntpublishing.com
www.christian-alternative.com

For distributor details and how to order please visit the 'Ordering' section on our website.

Text copyright: Roger Payne 2016

ISBN: 978 1 78535 482 3
978 1 78535 483 0 (ebook)
Library of Congress Control Number: 2016936946

A CIP catalogue record for this book is available from the British Library.

Design: Stuart Davies

Printed and bound by CPI Group (UK) Ltd, Croydon, CR0 4YY, UK

We operate a distinctive and ethical publishing philosophy in all
areas of our business, from our global network of authors to
production and worldwide distribution.

CONTENTS

This book is dedicated to all those with whom I have had discussions over the years about issues which arise in this and in my previous book

Acknowledgements

I am grateful to all those who in various ways have knowingly or unknowingly contributed to this book. I have made reference to the use of quotations and other material where possible but there are inevitably narratives that are now so embedded in my other writings that it is no longer possible to identify them. I apologise to any who find material in this book which may have originated in their own writings and which has not been acknowledged.

This book has also been enriched by discussions with members of the Parish of Bushey and others either individually or in House Groups over the years and I am indebted to them.

Biblical passages are from the New Revised Standard Version (NRSV) of the Bible unless otherwise stated.

I have not used inclusive language in this book because it invariably becomes clumsy but in most cases references should be to both male and female gender.

Preface

This book follows closely on the publication of my previous book, *A Different Way: A Human Approach to the Divine,* in which I raised the issue of language and the meaning of words. I quoted from Marcus Borg's book, *Speaking Christian,* where he writes:

> Christian language has become a stumbling block in our time. Much of its basic vocabulary is seriously misunderstood by Christians and non-Christians alike. Big words like *salvation, God, Jesus* and *Bible* and collections of words like *the creeds, Lord's Prayer,* and *liturgies* have acquired meanings that are serious distortions of their biblical and traditional meanings (Borg, 2011:1).

It became clear during the writing of that book and has become clearer since, that another of the words where meaning needs reassessment is 'authority', particularly when applied to 'religious authority' and the Christian enterprise. Common usage of the word has become so far removed from New Testament meanings that a recovery is necessary.

The meaning of 'authority' like other 'big words' is not 'set in stone'. As I wrote in my previous book:

> For the philosopher Wittgenstein, language is simply a form of communication, and cannot have a status in its own right. All we can do is to use language as best we can to express what we believe to be true for us (Payne, 2015:22).

The aim of this book is to show that our perceptions of the word 'authority' must change if we are to be true to the message of Jesus. In particular we need to go back to the message of Jesus that 'authority' should be about 'service' not 'power'.

The situation is particularly acute as a 'crisis of authority' sweeps through western civilisation and with it a profound impact on the mission of the Christian Church. Unless we are able to detach the word 'authority' from its more negative aspects in common usage and convey a more positive meaning to the wider world then our teaching will drift further away from what Jesus actually taught.

Introduction

The challenge to all forms of authority has become particularly acute since the middle of the twentieth century and has had a profound impact on all aspects of society. It has affected relationships in the home, in local communities and in the world at large. It has tested parents as they seek to nurture their children. It has undermined the ability of teachers to manage their classes. It has forced the police to change their tactics. It has required hospitals to engage with patients. It has caused local and national politicians to amend legislation. Many of these changes have had positive outcomes but many others are negatively charged and some remain unresolved. Some issues of authority are not recognised or are simply ignored. Others are carelessly or insensitively handled. Some groups are in turmoil amongst competing voices of authority. Other groups suffer from arbitrary and imposed authoritarian solutions. This whirlwind of change has been rightly called a 'crisis of authority'.

Religious communities have not been immune from all this and in some ways the 'crisis of authority' has been more acute for those with a religious disposition. Although the crisis applies to all religious groups, the purpose of this book is to consider the problems facing the Christian community in particular and to offer some thoughts on possible solutions. The Christian Church has numerous authority structures within it and many of those with official appointments are seen to be in authority over its members. The notion of authority has been pivotal in theological and ecclesiological debates within Christianity throughout its history and it has been at the centre of some of the most significant disputes. The conservative nature of the Christian enterprise has made it difficult to effect change so that tensions remain and will continue to remain high.

The first chapter of this book examines the origins of the word 'authority' and considers what might be meant by 'religious authority'. The next three chapters review how and by whom power and authority has been exercised throughout history and how a 'crisis of authority' has developed. The next two chapters then consider how individuals respond to religious authority and why they respond as they do. The final chapter looks at particular aspects of religious authority like authoritarianism and funda-mentalism. The conclusion seeks to find a reference point for further debate in the common humanity of all those who call themselves Christian.

What is religious authority?

Introduction

In his book, *Authority, Leadership and Conflict in the Church*, Paul Avis describes the root meaning of the word 'authority' as:

> ...profoundly liberational and therapeutic. It stems from the Latin verb *augere*, to make increase, to cause to grow, to fertilize, to strengthen or enlarge. This gave the noun root *auctor*, a doer, causer, creator, founder, beginner or leader. The senses of enabling and nurturing are fundamental – *auctoritas* meaning weighty counsel: more than advice and less than command (Avis, 1992:19).

On the face of it, this positive understanding of the origins of the word 'authority' bears little resemblance to our rather more negative use of the word today. In view of the current 'crisis of authority' it is perhaps time to take a closer look at this word and to explore ways in which this original sense might be recovered.

The origins of the word 'authority'

In his book, *Authority*, E D Watt explores the origins of the word 'authority' from its original Latin meaning through its use in the Roman world to its common usage today. The root word in Latin is *auctoritas*. In the Roman world *auctoritas* was quite distinct from *potestas*, which is associated with power and control and *imperium*, which is associated with command and order:

> *Auctoritas* in Roman republican government was not a right to rule; it was something quite distinct from the rights, *potestas* and *imperium*, to issue lawful commands which were legally enforceable. Each civil official had the *potestas* or the *imperium*, limited in time and in scope, that went with his

office. Within these specified limits, his commands were legally binding. In addition he possessed *auctoritas*, personal influence. To the Senate, however, neither *potestas* nor *imperium* was ascribed, only *auctoritas*. It issued no commands with the force of law; indeed, it issued no commands at all, but only pronouncements in the form of advice – authoritative advice – to the civil officials in whose hands executive power lay (Watt, 1982:12).

In the Christian tradition, both *auctoritas* and *potestus* have been used in relation to God, the scriptures and the Church, but as Robert Murray points out in his essay, *Authority and the Spirit in the New Testament*, 'the normal word for 'authority' in the New Testament is *exousia*:

> ...the noun denoting the situation in which one is able, competent or permitted. While *exousia* can mean moral authority, the quality by which Jesus impressed people in contrast with the scribes' cautious recital of past opinions, normally the best English equivalent for it is 'competence', the state of freedom to act, either in virtue of personal possession of a right or in virtue of authorisation by someone who has such a right and can communicate it to others. The New Testament concept expressed in the word *exousia* does not have the connotation of jurisdiction over others, much less the power to impose force on other persons, but rather the holder's rightful freedom to act (Murray, 1968:32-33).

In his book, Avis explains the significance of *exousia* in the distinction between authority and power in the practice of the Christian Church:

> In the New Testament it is *exousia* that legitimates *dynamis*. Mere dynamic phenomena are not spiritually significant or

theologically valid. The exousia of God and his Christ are not enforced by dynamic coercion, except in some eschatological scenarios, but are open to being freely acknowledged and willingly obeyed. The temptation for the Christian Church, as an institution, as an *imperium* even, has always been to take the short cut to mere power and to forget that the true substance of power, without which it is bankrupt and discredited, is the *exousia*, the 'moral authority' that it receives from God through the Christ whose authority did not prevent him from being nailed to a cross (Avis, 1992:20).

So, it is clear that the etymology of the word 'authority' is not straightforward. Watt concludes his account as follows:

Authority, then is a word with a range of meanings considerably broader than its Latin original... This seems to have been the case for as long as the English word has been used. So it is clear at the outset that to consider authority is to consider a group of ideas and not a single idea: to distinguish the more important of these ideas from one another, and to show, where it can be shown, how they are related (Watt, 1982:17).

The Concise Oxford Dictionary entries support this plurality of meaning in common English usage (Thompson, 1995).

The concept of 'authority' in common usage

'Authority' is a word that has both diversity and unity in its common usage. It describes a wide range of different kinds of authority, but all of these meanings of the word have something in common. At the start of his analysis in, *The Nature and Limits of Authority*, Richard De George suggests a 'working model of authority which handles the more obvious cases' which can then be 'expanded, refined, revised, and corrected as needed'.

> Someone or something is an authority if he (she, or it) stands
> in relation to someone else as superior stands to inferior with
> respect to some realm, field, or domain (De George, 1985:14).

De George goes on to make a first major distinction in ordinary usage between, what he calls 'executive authority', where authority 'has the right or power to act for or on someone else', and 'non-executive authority' which does not. Other writers describe the same distinction in different ways. R S Peters, for example, uses 'in-authority' and 'an-authority', which are perhaps more descriptive of how the word is actually used (Peters, 1970).

Further distinctions can be made. Non-executive authority can be further divided into 'epistemic authority', which is authority held on the basis of knowledge, and 'exemplary authority', which is authority held on the basis of example. Executive authority can be divided into 'natural authority' which arises from natural qualities such as leadership or strength, and 'conventional authority' which derives from a particular office or position. Although non-executive authority is perhaps less tangible than executive authority it plays an important role and enables complex societies to function. It is often the basis for conferring executive authority. These various distinctions can be illustrated within the different realms of authority. Political authority, for example, is primarily about the executive authority of those who hold office in government and its agencies. Religious authority can claim examples from all these distinctions. However, for those with a religious disposition, there is something unique in the authority of God.

For Max Weber, it is 'the kind of claim to legitimacy typically made' by each type of authority that distinguishes them. Legal-rational authority derives from 'a belief in the legality of patterns of normative rules and the right of those elevated to authority under such rules to issue commands'. Traditional authority derives from 'an established belief in the sanctity of immemorial traditions and the legitimacy of the status of those exercising authority under them'. Charismatic authority derives from 'a devotion to the specific and exceptional sanctity, heroism or exemplary character of an individual person, and of the normative pattern or order revealed or ordained by him' (Weber, 1964:325).

If authority is to be effective then it must not only have legitimacy but also power, and it is possible to have one without the other. A *de jure* government in exile may have authority but no power. The *de facto* rulers of the country may have power but no authority. But the distinction between legitimacy and power can become more complicated. A schoolteacher having difficulties with class discipline can carry authority from the school's point of view but lack authority with the pupils. Similarly, a priest may carry the authority of the bishop but not with parishioners. In both cases, power is lacking so authority is impotent.

The distinctiveness of 'religious authority' in the Christian tradition

In his book, *Authority: A Philosophical Analysis*, R Baine Harris writes:

> Of the four main historical types of authority: civil, moral, scientific, and religious, the last one has received the greatest challenge in modern times. Numerous historical and social factors are involved in this challenge, not least of which is the widespread difference of opinion concerning the *meaning* of religious authority itself (Baine Harris, 1976:132).

For those within the Christian tradition, God is the ultimate source of all authority. As traditionally understood, God created the universe and established the laws of nature. He also created human beings as part of that creation and continues to exercise authority over them.

> By recognizing or acknowledging God's dominion over them,
> human beings make God a *de facto* executive authority...
> However, divine authority is not religious authority. Divine
> authority is exercised by God; whatever religious authority
> turns out to be, it is exercised by human beings (De George,
> 1985:218).

What we can call 'religious authority' arises in both individuals
and in groups and arises in different ways. Christianity involves
communities of believers, who are bound together by their
common beliefs, joint practices, and some organisational
structure. Within those groups there will be bishops, priests and
deacons who have executive authority by virtue of their office.
There will be others who have non-executive authority by virtue
of their knowledge or example. It may well be that the non-
executive and less tangible aspects of authority which
individuals and groups have will ultimately be the most significant for the flourishing of the faith at any particular time or in
any particular place. But how is that authority legitimised?

> Religious authority comes from God, is exercised by human
> beings in the context of a church or religion, and is limited to
> religious matters – usually questions of belief in God, man's
> relation to God, the actions derived from these beliefs, and the
> morality implied by or contained in them. Just as belief in God
> is central to religion, so the basis and justification for religious
> authority is found in religious faith or in belief in God and his
> revelation (De George, 1985:219).

The major source for the notion of religious authority in the
Christian tradition is the Bible. In the Old Testament, all forms of
authority rested in religious authority and therefore ultimately in

God. In later periods, the different forms of authority become distinctive and established on their own terms, but the tensions between the various forms were resolved in some places and at some times better than others. The history of the relationship between these forms in Western Europe is similar but, according to Baine Harris, 'the exact function of religious authority was never settled in the Christian West'. He identifies three different issues that have led to the confusion concerning the meaning of the concept of 'religious authority.

> The first is the battle to separate civil, moral, and scientific authority from any dependency upon a religious base. The second is the conflict between the Church and the State for the control of society. The third is the debate that has gone on... concerning the criteria that should be used in the authenticating of religious meaning (Baine Harris, 1976:134).

The most important distinction, however, that can be made between the various ways in which religious authority is understood is that between 'ultimate religious authority', that is God, and the 'representative religious authority' of individuals. Since religious authority can be vested not only in individuals but also in groups, and not only in people but in texts and traditions, the definition of religious authority must be wider. It can also be extended to include, not only 'extrinsic authority', that is, authority arising from outside, but also 'intrinsic authority', that is, the authority that arises for an individual from within himself. It follows from this that the representative religious authority's most important quality is the extent to which he (she, or it) is 'transparent to the deity'.

Historically, there have been four finals appeals in the verification of religious authority – reason, experience, scripture and tradition – and a battle has raged and continues to rage about each of them. With this in mind, it is possible to trace the various ways in which people, texts and traditions have been considered to be 'transparent to the deity', and it is a complicated story. It starts with the distinction between 'revelation' and 'reason'.

The traditional distinction between 'revelation' and 'reason'

Christians have understood two sharply contrasting ways in which men and women learn about God. Revelation has traditionally been understood in terms of this distinction between revealed and rational knowledge.

Based on their interpretation of John's Gospel, both Augustine and Aquinas understood revelation as 'divine illumination'. In his essay entitled *Revelation*, George Stroup describes how, in his commentary on John's Gospel, Augustine:

> ...sounded a theme that is to be found throughout his theological writing: the identification of Jesus Christ as the light which illumines the darkness of the human intellect and overcomes the blindness created by human sin (Stroup, 1983:92).

In Augustine's writing, the distinction between the roles of revelation and reason is unclear. In Aquinas, however, a synthesis is achieved in which the two are understood as 'distinct but complimentary realms of understanding'. In his book *The Idea of Revelation in Recent Thought*, John Baillie writes:

> Aquinas would tell you on the one hand of 'an ascent, by the natural light of reason, through created things to the knowledge of God', and on the other of 'a descent, by the mode of revelation, of divine truth which exceeds the human intellect, not as demonstrated to our sight but as a communication delivered for our belief, (Baillie, 1956:4).

This synthesis did not last, and by the time of the Reformation, revelation and reason were firmly separated. This happened because views about the importance of one or the other became polarised. The Rationalists placed greater emphasis on reason, with some denying that any knowledge of God was possible without unaided powers of reason. The Reformers argued that human reason was so corrupted by sin that only revelation through scripture could yield reliable knowledge of God. For Luther, the Word of God is Jesus Christ and we only have access to that Word through the words of proclamation and scripture. But Luther does not simply identify the Word of God with the external words of proclamation and scripture. These words only become God's Word when the Spirit 'enables the external words to become internal words'. The Word and Spirit can therefore not be separated. The Roman Catholics took a different view. They argued that revelation took place through both the words of scripture and the traditions of the church.

Stroup describes how in the late sixteenth and early seventeenth centuries both models of revelation – Divine Illumination and Word and Spirit – were given objectivist interpretations by both Reformers and Catholics:

> In both cases, revelation referred to a series of propositions which were understood to be objectively true because they were taught by a divinely inspired church or could be found in a book authored by God (Stroup, 1983:96).

As Stroup also points out, it was inevitable that as the intellectual climate changed these positions would be challenged. In the event, both classical modes of revelation were 'shaken at their foundations' by the Enlightenment.

The period from the seventeenth to the nineteenth century was not only a period during which particular developments took place, but it was also a period during which a paradigmatic shift in intellectual thought occurred. The rise of science and the distrust of tradition were just two examples of a movement in which every proposition became subject to rational examination.

The Enlightenment insisted on 'reason' as the primary capacity of human beings and as the ultimate authority and judge for all religious claims. As a result, some thinkers tended towards atheism because of this new emphasis on the rational side of human nature. Others tended towards Deism in an attempt to accommodate the new approach by belief in a god who could be known by reason rather than revelation. Yet others rejected the claims of reason altogether and argued more strongly in favour of a faith based on revelation. Those who remained in the mainstream began to question previously accepted approaches to both scripture and tradition. They came to understand the importance of historicity, and from the Renaissance onwards, scholars applied historical-critical methods both to biblical and doctrinal issues. It became clear that individuals, communities and institutions were conditioned by their social and cultural contexts and what made sense at one time and in one place might not necessarily apply in another. Authority came to be associated more with the autonomy of individual responses to knowledge of God than with obedience to an imposed command.

Despite these changes, arguments between Catholics and Protestant churches about the relative importance of scripture and tradition as means of revelation continued to dominate the debate.

The historical tension between scripture and tradition

Scripture was at the centre of the life of the Early Church. It provided the raw material for proclamation of the gospel, it enabled people to respond to questions and attack and it sustained the church in its task. Scripture was a vital tool in fight against the paganism of the Greco-Roman world and the heresies of Marcion and the Gnostics in the first few centuries. In his book,

Scripture and the Authority of God, Tom Wright sums it up when he writes, 'The study of the early church as the scripture-reading community is one of the best ways of getting right to the heart of what early Christianity was all about'.

> Scripture furnished the church with the wherewithal for the proclamation and living of the Kingdom. It sustained the church in prayer and holiness. It enabled the early Christians to respond to questions and attacks. The challenge of Marian and the Gnostics to a radical reconfiguration of Christianity was met with a fresh appeal to scripture itself (Wright, 2005:45).

Although much was gained from reading scripture at 'face value', from the second century onwards a tradition of allegorical interpretation emerged.

> At its heart, allegory reads the surface text as a code through which hidden meanings may be discerned... Perhaps the best known example of the allegorical reading of scripture is the use of the love poem, the Song of Songs, as an allegory of the love between Christ and the church, in parallel with Jewish readings about the love between YHWH and Israel. What the use of allegory highlights, of course, is the church's insistence on the importance of continuing to live with scripture, including the bits which appeared deeply problematic – for example some of the more shocking stories in the Old Testament (Wright, 2005:49).

Such interpretation could provide valuable insights, but at the same time could become completely detached from the original text and highly imaginative. As a result, a tension arose between the authority of the original text and the authority of any inter-pretation of that text. By the medieval period such allegorical interpretations had become highly developed. They had also become one of the 'four senses' of interpretation – literal, allegorical, anagogical and moral.

> By the 'literal' sense they meant the original meaning – which, confusingly, might itself include allegory, or metaphor. The 'allegorical sense was the discovery of Christian doctrine within a passage whose original meaning did not seem to have anything to do with it: thus, for instance, Abraham's sending of his servant to find a bride for his son in Genesis 24, could be read as an allegory of God sending the gospel to find a bride for the church. The 'anagogical' sense was a way of discovering in the text a picture of the future life: perhaps the best known example of this would be the use of Psalms which speak of going up to Jerusalem as a way of referring to the Christian's destination in the heavenly city. ('Anagogical' means 'leading upwards'). The 'moral' sense was a way of discovering lessons on how to behave within texts which were not straightforwardly teaching such a thing (Wright, 2005:51).

In parallel with the authority claimed for the Bible, the church was increasingly claiming authority as the guardian of a developing tradition:

> By the sixteenth century a position had been reached which regarded 'tradition' as the essential supplement to, and indeed interpretive framework for, the Bible. This meant that anything which could be regarded as well established in ecclesial tradition, even if there was nothing about it in the Bible, and even if it appeared to go against some of the things which the Bible itself said, could be taught as authoritative and backed up with clever allegorical exegesis. (The perpetual virginity of Mary would be a good example.) (Wright, 2005:53).

Alongside this claim of authority by the church was its exercise of power. Power was exercised not only in the interpretation of scripture but also in the proclamation of dogma. The church had over the centuries built a massive ecclesiastical organisation with a huge framework of theology and doctrine. The growth of this vast edifice of power and influence, with the inevitable accusations of corruption and excess, and its increasing claims of extra-biblical authority were major causes of the Reformation.

The slogan of the Reformers was *sola scriptura* and their aim was the recovery of the 'literal' sense of scripture 'over against the lush growth of the other three senses':

> Go back to scripture, they insisted, and you will find the once-for-all death of Jesus but not the Mass, justification by faith but not purgatory, the power of God's word but not of the Pope. Their insistence that scripture contains all things necessary to salvation was part of their protest against the Roman insistence on belief in dogmas like transubstantiation as necessary articles of faith. It was never a way of saying that one had to believe every single thing in the scriptures in order to be saved (Wright, 2005:53).

Wright argues that the Reformers 'set scripture over against the traditions of the church' but, although they 'refused to regard non-biblical tradition as a *separate* authoritative source, they regularly appealed to the Fathers, demonstrating their own continuity with earlier, pre-medieval times and interpretations'. He concludes that:

> ...they wanted to insist that they stood in line with the best that had gone before, but never developed ways of explaining how that totality, the combination of scripture and the history of what the church had said as it read scripture, might fit together (Wright, 2005:55).

The official position of the Roman Catholic Church from the Council of Trent (1845-1863) onwards has been that scripture and tradition are of equal authority. In practice, however, it has claimed authority for statements that have no basis in scripture – papal infallibility for example. It has always been the Protestant position that scripture must always remain as the final test of which traditions are genuine interpretations of scripture and which are not.

Continental Reformers and Roman Catholics were not, however, the only protagonists in this heated and sometimes violent debate. English Protestants had their own battle to wage. Puritans argued that since scripture alone was authoritative, only those customs and practices explicitly authorised by scripture should be allowed. Many in the English Church took a different view.

Anglican perspectives on religious authority

Anglicans have always had a distinctive 'take' on religious authority, and much of the credit for this must go to the sixteenth century churchman Richard Hooker. Nigel Voak, in his recent book, *Richard Hooker and Reformed Theology*, writes:

The traditional view is that Hooker articulated, and was possibly the originator of the idea that there exists a triple source of religious authority: scripture, reason, and tradition, in that order. On the vexed topic of Anglican identity numerous writers have seen this theory of authority as central to Anglican self-understanding... (Voak, 2003:251).

During the turmoil of the sixteenth century, Hooker sought to find a middle way, between the Puritans, and their insistence on the Bible as the only source of divine authority, and the Catholics claim that the Bible must be supplemented by the tradition of the Church. His solution was to embrace both scripture and tradition, together with reason, as ways in which God's authority is mediated, and to argue for a fresh understanding of these elements and the relationship between them. He also issued a warning:

> Against both the Roman Catholics with their appeal to the infallibility of the church and of the pope, and the puritans with their biblical absolutism, Hooker insisted that the highest form of certainty we enjoy is that of 'probable persuasions'. Though the human mind craves 'the most infallible certainty which the nature of things can yield, assent must always be proportionate to the evidence. Neither direct intuition of supernatural truth nor demonstrative proof of them is given to humanity in its earthly pilgrimage (Avis, 2014:116-117).

Although, for Hooker, the scriptures were not an infallible guide to every aspect of life, they were the only source of knowledge that Christians must believe in order to be saved. They were therefore placed first in the hierarchy of sources. However, beyond the biblical message of salvation, the application of reason is necessary in order to understand our divinely implanted faculty for understanding the truth. The third component in Hooker's scheme is 'tradition' and he concedes that when appeals to scripture and reason are not decisive, the authority of the Church itself may be invoked.

In summing up Hooker's approach, Paul Avis writes, 'What distinguishes Hooker's use of authority in matters of religion is the absence of literalism and legalism'.

> Neither scripture nor tradition contains a set of binding prescriptions and precedents for the life of the church. Underlying his teaching on this question is the assumption that there is an intuitive moral and aesthetic discernment that judges what is appropriate in the circumstances, a sense of what is fitting, what is becoming (Avis, 2014:127-128).

Although Anglicans may argue over Hooker's particular understanding of the role of scripture, reason and tradition, most would probably embrace the comprehensiveness and pragmatism of his approach. Present tensions in the worldwide Anglican Communion, however, signal a rift in this consensus.

Modern understandings of 'revelation'

The legacy of the Enlightenment was a climate in which fresh thinking about theology in general and revelation in particular became possible. In the nineteenth and twentieth centuries a number of alternative understandings were proposed, from the views of Friedrich Schleiermacher (1768-1834) at one end of the spectrum to the views of Karl Barth (1886-1968) at the other.

Schleiermacher claims that after the Enlightenment, 'all theological assertions must be empirically grounded'. For him, that empirical grounding is found in religious experience. 'He believes, with the Romantics, that intense aesthetic experience, rather than the realm of cognition or action, is the locus of human perception of the truth of reality'.

For Schleiermacher, God is known immediately (that is, intuitively) in religious experience. There is a universal human sense of being completely dependent on God for our existence. In Christianity this sense of absolute dependence receives a Christological form, being shaped by the person and work of Jesus Christ and experienced only through the community that derives from him, the Church. This revelation is not propositional, but experiential, for doctrines are deduced from communal experience (Avis, 1997:48).

Karl Barth, 'denies that there is a universal religious experience, such as the sense of absolute dependence, on which Christian theology can build its specific claims'.

Human subjectivity provides no firm basis for theological construction, being fallen, corrupt and prone to idolatry. The only sound basis for theology is the word of God which is given, objective and coherent. Revelation is conveyed through the witness of Holy Scripture. The Bible is not identical with the word of God but attests it (Avis, 1997:49-51).

Whereas, Schleiermacher gives priority to the human capacity to experience God, Barth gives absolute priority to God's action and command. We do not decide what counts as revelation; we merely accept what is given.

If Schleiermacher and Barth represent opposite ends of the spectrum, there are others who occupy the middle ground or who adopt a different perspective. Some modern theologians have turned their attention to history as the proper sphere for understanding revelation. In his essay, *Revelation*, George Stroup claims that:

...what really gives rise to the prominence of revelation in modern theology is the emergence of critical history and with it the problem of hermeneutics' (Stroup, 1983:109).

The contemporary discussion of 'narrative theology' is one way in which revelation might be interpreted in these terms. Although narrative theology is indebted to both Schleiermacher and Barth, it is H Richard Niebuhr's (1894-1962) development of the category of 'story' or narrative 'that has most decisively influenced narrative theology's reinterpretation of revelation'.

Narrative Theology

In, *Christian Theology: An Introduction*, Alister McGrath writes:

Narrative Theology is based on the observation that the Bible tells stories about God, just as much as it makes doctrinal or theological statements. For example, the Old Testament could be said to be dominated by the telling and retelling of the story of how God led Israel out of Egypt into the Promised Land, and all this implies for the people of God. In a similar way, the New Testament is... also dominated by a story of God's redeeming action in history, this time centering on the life, death and resurrection of Jesus Christ (McGrath, 1997:200).

He goes on to suggest that for some, a major impetus was given to the Narrative Theology movement by H Richard Niebuhr's *The Meaning of Revelation'* (Niebuhr, 2006).

Niebuhr's constant emphasis upon the revelation of God in history led him to note that narratives were an especially appropriate way of expressing that revelation. God chose to become revealed in history and historical forms. The literary form most appropriate to represent that revelation was thus a narrative – a story. (The word 'story', it must be stressed, does not imply a 'work of fiction'). (McGrath, 1997:201).

In his book, *The Meaning of Revelation*, Niebuhr points out that narrative theology goes beyond the biblical stories to the stories that Christians throughout history have told about a deep personal relationship:

Interpretation of our meaning with the aid of a story is a well-known pedagogical device. So Lincoln told his homely tales and conveyed to others in trenchant fashion the ideas in his mind; so Plato employed myths to illustrate philosophy and to communicate visions of truth that ordinary language could not describe; so Jesus himself through parables tried to indicate what he meant by the phrase 'kingdom of God'. Yet what prompted Christians in the past to confess their faith by telling the story of their life was more than a need for vivid illustration or for analogical reasoning. Their story was not a parable which could be replaced by another; it was irreplaceable and untranslatable. An internal compulsion rather than free choice led them to speak of what they knew by telling about Jesus Christ and their relation to God through him (Niebuhr, 2006:25).

There is therefore something unique about the stories of narrative theology. And there is something unique about the perspectives that they bring to the nature of revelation itself. But they only go so far. It is time for even more imagination in the possibilities of new perspectives on revelation.

Religious Experience

In an article in *Modern Believing*, the journal of Modern Church, Paul Badham argues that compared with scripture, tradition and reason, 'individual religious experiencing is often treated as of little or no importance'. He goes on:

> This seems to me to be a profound mistake because if one explores the basis on which claims to revelation are made, one finds that religious experiencing lies at their heart. One of the most influential books on religious experience is Rudolf Otto's work, *The Idea of the Holy* (Otto, 1968). In this almost all the key examples of the numinous experience were derived from biblical accounts of human responses to the divine. In other words when one looks at the biblical material it becomes clear that so far from revelation being an alternative to religious experience, revelation is the supreme instance of religious experiencing (Badham, 2005).

Badham points out that an important theme in the writings of Friedrich Schleiermacher, the so-called 'Father of Modern Theology', is that reading the biblical accounts can awaken the reader's own religious sensibilities. He also shows that it is not just liberals in the Schleiermacher tradition who appeal primarily to human experience. 'This is also in practice true of evangelical Christianity'. He goes on:

> In theory evangelicals claim to believe in their version of Christianity on the basis of the authority of the Bible, but if one examines their preaching, their praying and the hymns they sing, it becomes clear that the real grounds for faith are personal religious feelings (Badham, 2005).

The pioneer of experimental research into religious experience was the Harvard Psychologist, William James (1842-1910). His book, *The Varieties of Religious Experience*, 'remains one of the finest anthologies of human religious experience as well as a brilliant discussion of its nature and provenance'.

This work was taken forward by the publication of Rudolf Otto's book, *The Idea of the Holy*, in which Otto (1869-1937) uses the phrase 'numinous experience' to 'identify the essential element at the heart of the awareness of a sacral presence'. The most important further development in the academic study of religious experience came when Sir Alister Hardy founded the Religious Experience Centre in Oxford in 1969. In, *The Spiritual Nature of Man*, Hardy (1896-1985) draws upon thousands of first-hand accounts of experience that the centre collected from individuals over a number of years.

In more recent research, David Hay and others have shown that more than 75% of the British population now claim an awareness of 'something other' in their lives despite the fact that less than 10% regularly attend church. This shows that, what can perhaps best be described as, 'spirituality' is still a very significant factor and claims some authority in people's lives. Contemporary research by Linda Woodhead, Professor of the Sociology of Religion at Lancaster University shows a further shift, but that is, sadly, beyond the scope of this book.

Conclusion

This brief review of the nature of religious authority reveals the potential for tension between those who promote the different sources of that authority. It also exposes the danger of its misuse as authority becomes power. In the next chapter we shall examine who or what exercised authority in the early years of the Christian Church. In subsequent chapters we will explore how authority became power and how power became crisis.

Who exercised religious authority in the early years of the Christian Church?

Introduction

In the previous chapter, we explored the notion of religious authority and the various ways in which it is understood. We briefly examined the role of scripture, tradition, reason and experience in the mediation and representation of that authority. We recognised the most important quality of representative authority as the extent to which he, she or it, is 'transparent to the deity'.

In this second chapter, we shall examine representative authority in more detail by identifying who or what exercised such authority in the early years of the Christian Church. In the third chapter we shall examine how that authority became power in later years and how that power was both used and abused.

God

In his essay, *God*, Langdon Gilkey outlines classic and contemporary understandings of, what he calls, the 'idea of God'. He describes it as 'at once the most important and yet the most questionable of all religious doctrines or symbols in the West'. He goes on:

> This idea or symbol points to the central object of both Christian and Jewish faith, the sole subject of their revelation, and the final principle of both reality and meaning throughout human existence. Nevertheless, of all concepts in modern cultural life the idea of God remains the most elusive, the most frequently challenged, the most persistently criticised and negated of all important convictions (Gilkey, 1983:62).

For the purposes of this book, it is not necessary to explore the various understandings of 'the idea of God' in the contemporary world, but it is necessary to acknowledge that when we speak about God we mean different things to different people. It follows that in order to proceed we must agree on an understanding of the idea of God that commands widespread respect and which is consistent with what follows. Furthermore, it must be an understanding that can accommodate the notion of authority that has already been developed.

In traditional Christianity, God is understood as the one Supreme Being, the focus of ultimate reality, the creator and sustainer of the universe. God is the ultimate source of all life, love and goodness in the world. God is a personal being taking an interest in the lives of each and every one. God has become incarnate in the person of Jesus so divinity has entered into humanity. God should be the object of worship, praise and prayer.

Such a statement is not without its difficulties, but it represents the view of many who would describe themselves as traditional Christians. For them, the notion of God's authority is not a problem. The way in which that authority is mediated, however, is much more contentious.

Jesus

The New Testament is our principle source of historical evidence for the person of Jesus and at the outset we must distinguish between perceptions of his divine and his human authority.

The New Testament was written against a background of the strict monotheism of Israel and it would have been blasphemous for anyone to be described as 'God' in this context. However, there are passages where Jesus is described as God. John's gospel opens with the words, 'In the beginning was the Word, and the Word was with God, and the Word was God (John 1:1). Later in the same gospel, in what Raymond Brown describes as the 'highest Christological confession in the Gospels' (Brown,

1997:360), Thomas exclaims, 'My Lord and my God' (John 20:28). In other parts of the New Testament, Jesus is described as having the attributes of God. Jesus saves us from our sins. 'She will bear a son, and you are to name him Jesus, for he will save his people from their sins' (Matt 1:21). Jesus is worshipped. 'To those who... in every place call on the name of our Lord Jesus Christ' (1Cor 1:2). Jesus reveals God. 'Whoever has seen me has seen the Father' (John 14:9). There is little doubt that for John and other New Testament writers, Jesus was either equal to or at least somehow 'transparent to the deity'. However, the relationship between Jesus and God was not easily settled for the church as a whole and this issue continued to divide the church for many centuries to come. However, these issues, though important, would prove to be a distraction if we were to pursue them here.

The New Testament accounts not only tell us what was said by Jesus and his disciples, but also the impression they made on the people listening to Jesus. 'They were astounded at his teaching, for he taught them as one having authority, and not as the scribes' (Mark 1:22). 'They were all amazed, and they kept on asking one another, "What is this? A new teaching – with authority! He commands even the unclean spirits, and they obey him."' (Mark 1:27). It was not necessary for Jesus to assert his authority in the company of those sympathetic to him. However, there were those who challenged that authority in defence of their own position. 'As he was walking in the temple, the chief priests, the scribes, and the elders came to him. "By what authority are you doing these things? Who gave you this authority to do them?" (Mark 11:27-28). In the ensuing exchange, divine authority is intimated, but it is not claimed.

The impression that Jesus made on his hearers was clearly profound and had as much to do with his humanity as any notion of divinity. It is clear from the gospel accounts that Jesus had a strong personality and an attractive disposition. He was a powerful speaker and a persuasive teacher. He was kind and generous in his dealings with those around him. At the same time, he could be provoked to anger, 'And he entered the temple and began to drive out those who were selling and those who were buying in the temple...' (Mark 11:15). He could be led to despair, as on the cross, '"My God, my God, why have you forsaken me?"' (Mark 15:34). In other words, Jesus was a real man, whatever else he may have been. It is enough to believe that he was supremely 'transparent to the deity'. Further speculation about his divine status is really not productive.

The Apostles of Jesus

The word 'apostle' comes from the Greek word *apostolos* which means one who is 'sent forth' or entrusted with a mission. It means rather more than 'messenger' and carries the implication of a 'delegate' or 'representative'. In the New Testament, its use implies an authority which derives directly from Christ. Its use is sometimes restricted to the twelve, but in other places it includes other named individuals like Paul and James who were specially 'called'. Sometimes it simply refers more generally to the disciples or followers of Jesus.

In his book, *Authority in the Apostolic Age*, R R Williams describes the twelve, with the exception of Judas, as 'the natural leaders of the Jerusalem Church', with 'some kind of authority or leadership over newer churches'. But, 'other leaders soon emerge – a James at Jerusalem, a Paul at Antioch and in the Gentile world. Seniority, a family link with Jesus, and probably a special meeting with the Risen Christ gave James his almost 'episcopal' place at Jerusalem: the fact of being the leading evangelist of the Gentiles gave Paul his place in the Gentile world'. He goes on:

An increasing reverence was due to the twelve as the first witnesses, but there is no suggestion that they are the sole sources of authority in the Church, and nothing to suggest that they were thought of as possessing a sole right of judgement or ordination after the earliest days. For this purpose, perhaps the wider idea of apostleship was more relevant (Williams, 1950:59).

The *de jure* authority of the twelve apostles has traditionally rested on their calling, their personal experience of Jesus and on their intimate knowledge of his life and teaching. It has also rested on gospel accounts of specific aspects of authority given to them by Jesus. 'Then Jesus summoned his twelve disciples and gave them authority over unclean spirits, to cast them out, and to cure every disease and every sickness' (Matt 10:1). Their *de facto* authority depended much more on their individual personalities and their effectiveness in communication of the gospel message. They were clearly a mixed bunch and the gospel accounts reveal a good deal about their individual strengths and weaknesses. Peter was impetuous. Thomas was sceptical. They were real human beings. Their *de jure* authority is therefore unquestionable, but their *de facto* authority is perhaps less clear.

Paul is a special case, for he claimed to be an apostle for quite different reasons. As far as we know he never met Jesus but he does claim that the resurrected Jesus appeared to him following his sudden conversion on the Damascus Road. He explains how Jesus first appeared to the other apostles then, 'Last of all, as to one untimely born, he appeared also to me' (1Cor 15:8). He claims authority as an apostle from his direct experience of the risen Jesus although he concedes that his previous persecution of Christians somewhat compromises his position. 'For I am the least of the apostles, unfit to be called an apostle, because I persecuted the church of God' (1Cor. 15:9). However, the tone of most of his writing is confident and assertive. He is sure of his ground.

The first letter to the Thessalonians is, by general consent, the earliest surviving Christian document. It was almost certainly written by Paul and it is undeniably about Paul and the assertion and defence of his authority in relation to people in the church of

Thessalonica. In his book *The Cost of Authority*, Graham Shaw examines the uses and abuses of authority in Paul's writing:

> In a lengthy passage he reminds them of his effectiveness, his sufferings, his courage; his freedom from error, uncleanness and guile, his divine authority and disinterestedness; his indifference to public opinion and his tireless industry (Shaw, 1983:30).

According to Shaw, Paul not only promotes himself directly but flatters and manipulates his followers in order to ensure that they continue to submit to his authority. He assures them that they 'became an example to all the believers in Macedonia and in Achaia... and not only in Macedonia and Achaia, but in every place your faith in God has become known' (1Thes 1:6-8). He commends their loyalty. 'For we now live, if you continue to stand firm in the Lord' (1Thes 3:8). He grants them privileges. 'For we know, brothers and sisters beloved by God, that he has chosen you (1Thes 1:4). But the granting of privileges implies imposition of obligation. They must 'lead a life worthy of God, who calls you into his own kingdom and glory' (1Thes 2:12). Paul is particularly vehement in his condemnation of gentile sexual practices. In other letters, Paul's authority comes under attack and he is forced to defend it vigorously. Shaw sums up his 'take' on these and other passages in the first letter to the Thessalonians as follows:

> The whole tone of the letter is assertive. As an example of Christian liberation and reconciliation it is not convincing: a small religious group bound up and manipulated by the self-esteem of the founder, gulled into submission by special privileges... (Shaw, 1983:32).

There are, of course, other ways to 'read' Paul, but for Shaw it is clear that in the very earliest Christian writings there is considerable evidence of both the use and the abuse of authority and power by those who, despite their status as respected Christians, were also vulnerable human beings. Although Paul does not confuse his authority with that of God, he seems, at times, to come very close. Paul's *de jure* authority may be uncertain but, judging by the influence of his writing on subsequent generations, his *de facto* authority is secure.

In his book, *Authority in the Apostolic* Age, R R Williams uses Paul's First Letter to the Corinthians to illustrate what he describes as 'the five main grounds of appeal to authority' which Paul uses in the epistle – the experience of the Corinthians at and after their conversion; the general stock of knowledge and accepted practice within the community; the oracles of the Old Testament 'newly interpreted'; Paul's own status and relationship with the community; and the moral welfare of the Church. In every case, however, it is the authority of Christ himself which is being exercised. It is difficult to overstate the case that, for Paul, the authority of Christ infuses everything. (Williams, 1950).

As the apostolic age receded, other ministers were appointed to preserve the apostolic witness as clear and undiluted and to deal with the practical and pastoral issues of an emerging church. The first bishops, priests and deacons appointed by the apostles themselves clearly carried their authority in a very special way. Thereafter, those appointed by sections of the church sometimes struggled to be accepted and issues of 'apostolic succession' loomed large in subsequent debate.

The Fathers of the Early Church

In his book, *Teaching Authority in the Early Church*, Robert Eno explains that the term "Fathers" is 'usually reserved for Christian writers marked by orthodoxy of doctrine, holiness of life, ecclesiastical approval and antiquity'. He goes on to say that the Fathers manifested a 'static' world view in which 'preservation of the treasures from the past is the keynote'. He adds, 'Nothing was to be added to doctrine; nothing subtracted from it'. The principal image was that of the 'deposit' (Eno, 1984:14).

One reason for this attitude was the classical tendency to look to the past and to concentrate on the unchanging core of teaching. Another was the need to preserve teaching in the face of persecution from the civil authorities and subversion from heretical movements within the wider community. The most insidious of those movements was Gnosticism.

In the first volume of *The Pelican History of the Church*, Henry Chadwick describes Gnosticism and its impact on the growing Church. He explains how the term Gnosticism is derived from the ordinary Greek word for knowledge – *gnosis*, and that members of the Gnostic sects claimed to possess a special knowledge which transcended the simple faith of the Church. He goes on to describe Gnosticism as 'an immense problem and threat to the Church as the personal authority of the first gener- ation of Christian leaders receded into the past' In his epistles, Paul writes against Gnostic tendencies which arose amongst Gentile converts.

In Corinth, a 'spiritual aristocracy' had emerged claiming 'profounder wisdom and deeper mystical experiences'. Members of this group were dualists who believed that 'the spirit is every- thing' and 'the body nothing'.

This belief had immediate moral consequences. Some Corinthians concluded that physical acts were a matter of indifference; taking encouragement from Paul's doctrine of freedom from the law, and regarding the sacraments as magical guarantees of automatic bliss, they fell into moral license. Rival groups adopted extreme ascetic opinions, so that husbands and wives withheld conjugal rights from one another and betrothed couples abstained from consummating their marriage (Chadwick, 1967:34).

At Colossae in Asia Minor Paul met with a graver heresy:

> ...a syncretistic amalgam of Christianity with theosophical elements drawn partly from the mystery cults and partly from heterodox Judaism. The Colossian Christians were being persuaded to worship intermediate angelic powers, identified with heavenly bodies, and believed to possess a power to determine human fate unbroken by the Gospel... (Chadwick 1967:34).

There seems little doubt that Paul's absence from these fledgling churches and the difficulties associated with appointing leaders who were necessarily not first generation apostles was a contributory cause of the problems that arose.

In addition to the threats from outside, there were threats from inside the Church. In particular, the Christian attitude to the Gentiles was an issue which caused deep division, the beginnings of which can be traced to the story of Stephen (d. c35) told by Luke in Acts 6-7.

Stephen was probably a Hellenistic Jew, that is, he spoke only Greek and probably came from the Diaspora, as opposed to those Jews who came primarily from Jerusalem and Judea and spoke a Semitic language in addition to Greek. It is fair to assume that the differences in language and origin would also lead to differences in outlook and attitude. Some Hellenists were quite content to abandon circumcision, food laws and some of the stricter demands of the more traditionally devout Jews. This inevitably led to the tensions which arose when the apostles appointed seven from this group, including Stephen, to look after the relief of the poor in the community. Quite apart from the details of the incident itself, and the subsequent death of Stephen, this incident demonstrates the first recognition by the apostles of the need for different kinds of ministry and the first evidence of their delegation of authority. The apostles reserved for themselves the primary tasks of preaching and teaching and delegated to 'the seven' the secondary tasks of supplying the basic human needs of food, clothing and shelter to those in need. Although the word 'deacon' is not used, this incident can be seen as a first step towards diaconal ministry in the Early Church.

Tensions also arise between Paul and the Jerusalem leadership over similar issues. In Galatians we read of the Jerusalem agreement.

> When they saw that I had been entrusted with the gospel for the uncircumcised, just as Peter had been entrusted with the gospel for the circumcised... they gave to Barnabas and me the right hand of fellowship, agreeing that we should go to the Gentiles and they to the circumcised (Galatians 2:7-9).

Soon after, we read of the incident in Antioch in which Paul accuses the Jerusalem group of undermining that agreement.

> But when Cephas (Peter) came to Antioch, I opposed him to his face, because he stood self-condemned; for until certain people came from James, he used to eat with the Gentiles. But after they came, he drew back and kept himself separate for fear of the circumcision faction... But when I saw that they were not acting consistently with the truth of the gospel, I said to Cephas before them all, "If you, though a Jew, live like a Gentile and not like a Jew, how can you compel the Gentiles to live like Jews?"' (Galatians 2:11-14).

The later Pastoral Epistles, and in particular the Letters to Timothy, give further evidence for the growing problem of doctrinal divergence.

> I solemnly urge you: proclaim the message; be persistent whether the time is favorable or unfavorable; convince,

rebuke, and encourage, with the utmost patience in teaching. For the time is coming when people will not put up with sound doctrine, but having itching ears, they will accumulate for themselves teachers to suit their own desires, and will turn away from listening to the truth and wander away to myths' (2Tim 4:1-4).

These writings also demonstrate the growing authority that was being invested in local leaders of the Church. They were seen as inheriting the apostolic tradition and upholding the deposit of faith.

Not surprisingly, the first century came to be seen as a very special period because of its close association with Jesus himself and with the Apostles and Fathers of the Early Church. This came to mean for some that this period was unique in the life of the Church and that divine revelation was confined within it. However, such an attitude was difficult to sustain as new questions arose and new difficulties were encountered. In the event, the 'deposit' was not as fixed as some would have wished because it could not have remained so and survived. This is particularly true in relation to questions about the status of Jesus. Christians prided themselves on being monotheists but needed to resolve the apparent paradox of Jesus as both human and divine. This was such a pressing issue that it dominated discussion and was only partially resolved in the great councils several centuries later. Despite the difficulties, however, the notion of a 'closed' revelation continued to dominate. The role of the leaders of the local churches as guardians of this revelation increased their authority and led eventually to the notion of the *magisterium*, or teaching authority of church, which we recognise in the Roman Catholic Church of more recent times. This *magisterium* reached its apogee in the Decree of Papal Infallibility of 1870.

In his book, *Teaching Authority in the Early Church*, Robert Eno draws a parallel between this *magisterium* and the ongoing interpretation by the Supreme Court of the Constitution of the United States. Not everyone, of course, would agree with these sentiments, but the parallel is not unreasonable. He writes,

The Founding Fathers of the United States of America could not have foreseen all the developments that have taken place in the world over the past two centuries. Some authoritative body has to exist to make decisions about ongoing laws and legal decisions in relation to the original Constitution' (Eno, 1984:20).

The first references to ministerial functions, other than apostles, occur in Paul's Epistles, and particularly in the First Letter to the Corinthians. 'And God has appointed in the church first apostles, second prophets, third teachers; then deeds of power, then gifts of healing, forms of assistance, forms of leadership, various kinds of tongues...' (1Cor 12:28). In a later chapter, Paul expands on the role of those with particular spiritual gifts and develops the idea of ministerial responsibility, particularly in relation to liturgy and worship... 'When you come together, each one has a hymn, a lesson, a revelation, a tongue, or an interpretation... Let two or three prophets speak, and let the others weigh what is said.' (1Cor 14:26-29).

The *Didache* or 'Teaching of the Twelve Apostles' is a document, probably Syrian, whose origins go back to the first century. It seems to have been written in a transitional period between the itinerant ministry of apostles, prophets and teachers and the more settled ministry of bishops, priests and deacons.

Therefore, ordain for yourselves bishops and deacons worthy of the Lord, meek men, not avaricious, truthful, chosen. They will also fulfill for you the work of the prophets and teachers. Do not look down on them, for they should be honored by you along with the prophets and teachers (Eno, 1984:32).

As the tradition of bishops, priests (or presbyters) and deacons developed in the first and second centuries, their roles needed to be clarified. As he was being escorted on his final journey to a martyr's death in Rome, Ignatius of Antioch (c35–c107) wrote to the churches which had helped him on his way. In his Letter to the Magnesians he writes:

> ...take great care always to act in God's concord, with the bishop who holds the place of God, with the presbyters, who are like the college of the Apostles, and with the deacons who are so dear to me, to whom Jesus' own special work has been entrusted... Let there be nothing among you to serve as an excuse for schism, but unite yourselves to the bishop and to those who preside... (Eno, 1984:34).

It is clear in this and other letters that Ignatius sees obedience to the bishop and the centralising of his authority as an important part of the fight against those forces which threatened to pull the church apart.

By the end of the second century, the acknowledged leaders of the local church were the bishops. Chadwick describes the relationship between a bishop and his presbyters as 'first among equals'. Presbyters had authority to celebrate the Eucharist and to discipline the faithful, but 'the presbyter inherited the lower role of the teacher, while the bishop inherited those of the apostle and the prophet' (Chadwick, 1967:50). Deacons were not ordained but had liturgical and administrative roles as assistants.

In his five books, *Against Heresies*, Irenaeus of Lyons (c115-190) argued that the Gnostic teachers were dangerous because 'they impelled Christians to leave the tradition transmitted in the apostolic succession' (Grant, 1997:6). The beginnings of this notion of 'apostolic succession' appear in a letter written by Clement of Rome (c96). Clement is traditionally considered to have been the third bishop of Rome after Peter and his authority seems to have extended well beyond Rome. At the end of the first century there was a revolution in the Corinthian Church in which old clergy were deposed and new clergy put in their place. In this letter, Clement calls on the Christian community in Corinth to reinstate the deposed clergy because they stand in due succession from the apostles even if they were not actually ordained by them. The letter seeks to establish a link between Christ, the apostles and later generations of church leaders and so to protect them from subsequent challenges to their leadership. This was particularly important in refuting the claims of the Gnostics that their special knowledge of the teaching of Jesus was obtained by alternative routes which bypassed apostles like Peter and Paul.

In the early church, authority was exercised not only by people but also by words. In the first century, the written words of the Old Testament and the spoken words of Jesus were authoritative. In the second, century, the oral tradition declined as the words of Jesus were written in the gospels. However, it did not disappear until it became unreliable in the face of the Gnostic threat. The synoptic gospels seem to have achieved general acceptance rather earlier than John's Gospel, the authority of which was disputed by some because of discrepancies. Other books earned their place only if they passed the test of apostolicity which meant that the Epistle to the Hebrews was initially excluded. The first New Testament canon, the Muratorian Canon, probably dating from the beginning of the second century and so called because it was first printed in 1740 by L A Muratori from an 8th century manuscript at Milan, specifically excludes those writings that were not considered apostolic. Although it is sometimes difficult to understand the decisions to include or exclude particular books, it is remarkable that the canon that we recognise today was so quickly established.

Authority was also given to the 'Rule of Faith', an early summary of the teaching of the Church used by Irenaeus and

Tertullian in their refutation of heresy. Although developed from the Bible, this early creedal statement was seen as a better defence against Gnosticism than the Bible itself because it was a clear statement of what the Church believed and was rather less prone to a range of alternative interpretations. It had apostolic authority because it contained the essence of what the bishops were currently teaching and was the raw material for their examination of baptismal candidates.

This can be seen as marking the beginning of a distinction between Scripture and Tradition as two distinct sources of revelation. However, this distinction is complicated by the fact that the one depends on the other for its authentication. As Chadwick points out:

> The argument is of course circular: the tradition of the Church teaching must be proved orthodox by the biblical revelation; yet doubtful books are admitted to the New Testament canon because they are orthodox by the standards of Church tradition, and only the tradition can ensure that the interpretation of Scripture is sound (Chadwick, 1967:45).

By the middle of the second century, the various Christian communities had become more 'settled' and there was increasing uniformity in both faith and order and, as Chadwick explains, 'the three-tiered system of one bishop in one city, with presbyters and deacons, was attained without controversy' He goes on:

> A further natural development was the provincial system by which in the third century special dignity came to be accorded to the bishop of the metropolis of the imperial province, and yet more transcendent honour to the bishops of the three great cities of the empire, Rome, Alexandria, Antioch, which are nominated in the sixth canon of the Council of Nicea (325), as possessing a jurisdiction beyond that of the civil province

(Chadwick, 1967:51).

Jerusalem was accorded a special place but it never became a centre of power in the Church because of the decline in influence of Jewish Christians. It was Rome that emerged as the 'natural leader' of the Christian West not least because of its role as the capital of the Gentile world and the part that it played in the development of the Early Church.

As the church grew there were disputes which could not be settled by the local church and increasingly bishops met together in councils to resolve problems. The Emperor Constantine was particularly attracted to this idea and in the fourth century presided over several councils (Arles 314, Nicaea 325) which sought to resolve particular problems. As the Western and Eastern Church emerged as quite distinct entities, we see, what Robert Eno calls:

...two divergent tendencies, the one, especially strong in the East, that looked to consensus and reception as the ultimate criteria in doctrinal questions. Here the general council would be the supreme expression of this consensus with the emperor enforcing its decisions. The Roman see came to view itself as superior to councils, that its tradition was apostolic without taint and therefore normative for the Church as a whole' (Eno, 1984:29).

By the third century Christianity had spread throughout the Roman Empire and, despite internal divisions and external threats, Christian communities had grown in towns and cities throughout the empire. Sometimes the external threats caused internal divisions as in the case of the persecutions by Diocletian at the beginning of the fourth century. In a major reorganisation, the empire was divided between two Augusti, each with an assistant Caesar. An edict was issued declaring that all churches were to be destroyed, all Bibles and liturgical books surrendered, all scared objects confiscated and all meetings forbidden. In due course all citizens were required to sacrifice to the emperor on pain of death. Inevitably, the severity of persecution varied, as did the response of those persecuted:

> As in modern times the Christians differed among themselves about the point at which resistance to the State must be absolute. In the East sacrifice was regarded as apostasy, not the surrender of sacred books and church plate. But in the West opinion was divided, passion ran high, and in consequence, although persecution was briefer and left most western provinces unaffected, the scars were more serious than in the East... The worst legacy of the persecution was once again schism (Chadwick, 1967:122).

The 'conversion' to Christianity of the Emperor Constantine following his victory over Maxentius at the Milvian Bridge in 312 had a major impact on the fortunes of the Christian Church. Although there has never been universal agreement about what this 'conversion' meant for Constantine himself, it is clear that the changing climate for Christians meant not only the end of state sponsored persecution but also the beginning of a far reaching partnership between Church and State. Reparations for the ravages of persecution were extensive with new Bibles commissioned and new churches built, and Christian sensibilities were accommodated in the legal and administrative reforms of the State. Financial provision for the running costs of the Church was generous. Constantine became sole ruler of the empire when he defeated Licinius on the Bosphorus in 324 and moved his capital to Byzantium and renamed it Constantinople. Although external threats had passed, internal divisions within the Church, and in particular the Arian controversy, preoccupied the emperor for some time to come.

The Council of Nicaea was convened by Constantine in 325 to deal with the fermenting crisis which had started as a local dispute between the presbyter Arius and his bishop Alexander of Alexandria but which now threatened the unity of the Church as a whole. This doctrinal dispute concerned the relationship between the Son and the Father, with Arius claiming that the Son had been created and was therefore different in kind from the Father. The council rejected this and adopted the statement that the Son is 'of one substance with the Father'. This seemed to favour those opposed to Arius but the statement was ambiguous. So, although Constantine had hoped that this statement would settle the matter, the dispute continued and dominated discussion for many years to come. It was at least a contributory factor in the final schism between the eastern and western branches of the Christian Church. As Frances Young puts it in her book, *From Nicaea to Chalcedon*:

On the one hand it (the Arian controversy) stimulated the discussions which led to the formulation of the Trinitarian dogma... on the other hand it shattered the unity of the church just as it acquired peace, power and influence in the empire, and it even exacerbated the unhappy state of the Catholic West when it fell a century later before the barbarian invaders – for the barbarians were converts to the Arian version of Christianity (Young, 1983:57).

By the end of the fourth century the Church had become firmly established in society. However, there were those within it who renounced possessions and the 'trappings' of normal life and aspired to a life of prayer and service to others. These ascetics had been around for some time but now with a church no longer under persecution their numbers increased. They also increasingly withdrew from ordinary congregations. This weakened individual churches and left those who had withdrawn without episcopal oversight. Some ascetics became members of settled communities, others travelled from place to place, while some became hermits, sometimes living in complete isolation. There were tensions between these various understandings of the monastic vocation, and disputes arose about the extent to which ascetics were pursuing individual or collective interests. There was also concern about the tendency of those not bound to established communities to drift away from orthodox teaching. The growth of such communities and the adoption of the *Rule of St Benedict* in the sixth century did much to allay those fears.

Divisions in the Church were apparent in the way authority and power were exercised in different parts of the empire. The Council of Nicaea retained its credibility throughout the empire, but subsequent councils carried less 'weight' because they suffered from the legacy of the Arian controversy. In the East, order and discipline continued to be exercised by the metropolitan bishops and by regional councils. In the West, however, it was the bishop of Rome who exercised that function and it was to him that all major issues were referred. The pre-eminence of the bishop of Rome had been growing for some time. From an early date, the bishop of Rome was regarded as 'first among equals'. This can be traced back to the importance of Rome as the 'centre of gravity' of the Gentile world, and to its role in the suppression of heresy during the second century. However, the fact that Rome was the only apostolic foundation in the West gave it special status long before its role was given 'authority' by reference to the reported words of Jesus:

And I tell, you are Peter, and on this rock I will build my church, and the gates of Hades will not prevail against it. I will give you the keys to the kingdom of heaven, and whatever you bind on earth will be bound in heaven, and whatever you loose on earth will be loosed in heaven' (Matthew 16:18-19).

From the time of Pope Damasus (366–383) onwards, pastoral letters became papal decrees, and a more centralised framework of order and discipline was imposed. The gap widened between the Latin and Greek churches and by the time of Pope Gregory the Great (590-604) the churches have effectively gone their separate ways.

Conclusion

It is clear from this account, that as the Christian Church grew in size and influence, it also claimed increasing authority and wielded greater power. What started in the Early Church as questions of the mediation of the authority of God became, in the Middle Ages, increasingly issues of power exercised by the Church. The abuse of that power was a major cause of The Reformation and it is to the abuse of that power that we must now turn.

Who or what exercised power from the Middle Ages to the Twentieth Century?

Introduction

The shift from 'authority' to 'power' is significant. In the early years of the Christian Church, questions of authority dominated debate as the number of those who claimed authority, because they were companions of Jesus, declined and the number of those claiming authority for different reasons increased. In later years, that authority became power and its use and abuse is the subject of this chapter.

The Western Church in the Middle Ages

In, *Western Society and the Church in the Middle Ages,* Richard Southern writes:

> The fall of the Roman Empire left a mental and spiritual as well as a political ruin which it took centuries to repair. The collapse was a long and complicated business, but in the West it was complete by the end of the seventh century. It was then that the work of rebuilding began. The dominating ideal in the rebuilding was that the unitary authority of the Empire should be replaced by the unitary authority of the papacy. (Southern, 1970:24).

He goes on:

> The identification of the church with the whole of organised society is the fundamental feature which distinguishes the Middle Ages from earlier and later periods of history... the church was a compulsory society in precisely the same way as the modern state is a compulsory society. Just as the modern state requires those who are its members by the accident of

birth to keep its laws, to contribute to its defence and public services, to subordinate private interests to the common good, so the medieval church required those who had become its members by the accident of baptism to do all these things and many others (Southern, 1970:16-17).

In many ways, therefore, the medieval church behaved like a state. However, despite the best efforts of the medieval popes, the church was never able to exercise the same authority. The authority of the state and the church arose from quite different sources. Furthermore, the church had no really effective means of enforcement. Its only weapon was excommunication, and enforcement relied on support from secular rulers. 'All systems of government depend ultimately on consent, and the medieval church came in the end to depend on the consent of a few secular rulers' (Southern, 1970:20).

By the beginning of the seventh century, there were already divisions between the Western and Eastern branches of the Christian Church but they were still part of a united Christian Empire. The advance of Islam and the need to defend Christian lands to some extent cemented this bond. However, political and doctrinal divisions, and the differences of custom and practice between Roman and Greek, eventually drove the two halves of Christendom apart. Although many of the popes in this period were Greek and had more in common with the peoples of the East than those of the West, the papacy eventually realised that its future lay in the other direction. The iconoclast movement in the East further alienated the Pope and encouraged him to look for Western rather than Eastern alliances. Such alliances led eventually to the coronation of Charlemagne by the Pope in 800 and the end of any semblance of political unity between West and East. Doctrinal unity was maintained for many years but with increasing difficulty. Eventually the tension became too great and the final split between West and East was inevitable.

This came in 1054 when the Pope excommunicated the Patriarch of Constantinople.

The unofficial addition of the *filioque* clause to the Nicaean Creed and its widespread use in the West was a major cause of division. The Western Church commonly uses a version of the Nicene Creed which has the Latin word *filioque* ("and the Son") added after the declaration that the Holy Spirit proceeds from the Father. This arose from the Arian controversy outlined in the previous chapter

The popes of the medieval period had more authority and power than at any other time in the history of the papacy. Initially, this authority arose from the certainty that the pope was the rightful successor of Peter and that the apostle's bodily presence in Rome somehow guaranteed the authenticity of that succession. For a long period, the presence of Peter was so strong that it was as if he was still alive and active in the affairs of men and women who sought to find him through their contact with the pope. However, in time the emphasis shifted as the pope started to call himself the 'Vicar of Christ' rather than the 'Vicar of Peter' in line with the need for a higher and more universal authority. The authority of the pope also arose from his claim to lordship over the temporal as well as the spiritual affairs of the people. This claim had some foundation but was frustrated by the emperor whom the pope had himself crowned. In practice, for most of the medieval period the emperor held the upper hand in temporal matters and the pope in matters spiritual. The power of both emperor and pope increased as they extended the machinery of government and appointed increasing numbers of people to act on their behalf.

Southern describes the main characteristics of the medieval ruler, whether secular or ecclesiastical as 'a dispenser of benefits and a dispenser of justice'. They were dispensers of benefits because 'it was the chief way in which a ruler could attract loyalty'. They were dispensers of justice because 'it was the only practical way in which they could enforce their lordship' (Southern, 1970:112-113).

The pope, although 'first amongst equals', was also a bishop. Inevitably, the roles of other bishops of the church also changed during the medieval period. Most noticeably they lost some of their independence as the pope increasingly intervened in what had previously seemed to be local matters. As Southern puts it,

> In all matters concerning the appointment discipline, trans-lation, or deprivation of bishops, the papal word was law; the local legislation of the bishops re-enacted the general legis-lation of the popes; their courts were wide open to papal directives coming down from above and to appeals to the pope rising from below (Southern, 1970).

But, he goes on to say that the bishops, 'gained in solidarity of purpose, in the protection of a supreme spiritual authority, and in fellowship in an immense common task' Substantial benefits accrued to the bishops in the expansion of papal power. It is important to note that the bishops were not faceless individuals. They were often wealthy men from powerful families whose position in the local community was well established and whose status was respected, even by the pope. They exerted consid-erable influence which extended far beyond their leadership of the local church. It seems that their personal qualities and their suitability as spiritual leaders rarely played much part in their appointment.

> The main centres of religious life in medieval Europe were communities specially endowed and set apart for the full, lifelong, and irrevocable practice of the Christian life... (Southern, 1970:214).

So Southern begins his chapter on the Religious Orders which rose to prominence in the Middle Ages. This is a bold claim but it is supported by evidence of a large number of 'religious' in communities of many different kinds 'all united in one respect: they had all taken life-long vows which set them apart from ordinary members of the church'. They 'varied in size and wealth, but even more strikingly in the purposes for which they had been founded and in their way of life'. Although members of these communities were 'set apart' from society, they were influenced by it to such an extent that 'the driving forces in their development were quite different from those of the original founders'. A tension therefore existed between 'a strong grasp on the things of this world, and an ardent desire for the rewards of eternity'(Southern, 1970:214-216).

The first of the western orders was the Benedictine Order. It was the greatest of the western orders and it provided an 'authoritative standard' for life in many of the religious communities of this time. The main element in the Rule of St Benedict is the practice of obedience, that is, obedience to God, to the Rule and to the Abbot. On the face of it, this seems to be a 'blind obedience' more in common with the parade ground than with the religious community. Yet this is not the case as will become clear in a discussion of 'obedience' as a response to 'authority' in a later chapter.

The Age of Reformation

As Owen Chadwick observes at the start of his book, *The Reformation*:

> At the beginning of the sixteenth century everyone that mattered in the Western Church was crying out for reformation (Chadwick, 1964:11).

This cry was primarily directed at the administrative, legal and moral weaknesses of the Church. There was little reference to a need for reformation of doctrine. The Pope was criticised, but for the inefficiency, incompetence, corruption and immorality within the Church, not for the promotion of false teaching.

At the beginning of the sixteenth century, the calls for change were not new but there was a new urgency. Previous attempts at reformation had often been attempts 'to put the clock back' and had largely been unsuccessful. Savonarola's abortive attempts to curb the excesses of papal power resulted in his execution in Florence in1498 as his supporters deserted him. His was no new vision of how things might be in the future; he wanted to go back to how things were in the past. As Chadwick puts it, 'His was the medieval cry for reform uttered in the old way, triumphant for a moment in the old way, suppressed in the old way' (Chadwick, 1964:22).

The new reformation was born in a world that was rapidly changing. Authority and power were shifting from Church to State and there was a new understanding of how that authority and power should be understood. Kings, princes and nobles variously asserted control over events and people within their own realm, and forms of governments that we associate with the modern nation-state began to emerge. In matters of both church and state, the role of the pope declined and the notion of Christendom was disappearing fast.

The intellectual climate was also changing. Following the discovery of printing and the expansion of libraries, more people were reading books. Knowledge was increasing as a new spirit of learning swept across Europe. There was a new understanding of what it meant to be human and a new appreciation of individual worth. The authority of people and institutions came under increased scrutiny. In Northern Europe this new movement took the form of Christian Humanism. Its most prominent member was Erasmus (c1466-1536) who laid the foundations for the refor-mation that was to follow.

In his study of Erasmus, James McConica gives some

background to the humanist movement at this time. He writes that the humanists were 'opposed to the established intellectual culture of the medieval university'. More generally, they were:

> ...absorbed with the place and potentialities of the human individual in this world, without excluding the perspective of an eternal destiny. These preoccupations reflected the needs of an increasingly urban and literate lay society, first in Italy, then in northern Europe. In classical antiquity they felt they found a distant but seemingly recognisable culture contrasting with that prevailing about them, and having a particular authority for the solutions of the questions they faced. It became urgent therefore to study the texts bequeathed by that culture, to master the languages which would give immediate access to them (McConica, 1991:6).

As a Christian humanist, Erasmus placed this enterprise firmly in the context of his commitment to the person and work of Jesus Christ and to God's revelation through scripture. His aim was not revolution. He wanted to reform medieval Christianity and to remove of all those things that had come to contaminate the Church and its message. His most powerful weapon was his pen which he wielded with scholarship and skill. He wrote with eloquence and wit and with 'coruscating satire'. His most famous work is, *In Praise of Folly*, which, according to Nicholas Lezard in a recent review, 'should be on every civilised bookshelf'. He goes on:

> The modern world begins, in a sense, with this book. Or at least the modern sense of humorous sceptical inquiry, a world in which the claims of dogma are countered by those of wit and good sense. You could say that we have regressed somewhat, at least in religious terms. There isn't a great deal of wit any more in Christianity (Lezard, 2008).

Erasmus did not seek controversy but consensus and was not comfortable with the divisions that emerged. He laid the foundations but has never been associated with any particular reformation movement. For this reason he is a somewhat lonely figure. James McConica calls him 'the Reformation's orphan' (McConica, 1991:1). According to Chadwick, it was said of the Reformation:

> Erasmus laid the egg and Luther hatched it (Chadwick, 1964:39).

That well describes the roles played by each of these men who had similar objectives but totally different approaches. They were both very able men but whereas Erasmus was a traditional scholar, Luther's scholarship was of a very different kind. It is tempting to describe their approaches as sophisticated and simple respectively. Luther had no time for the schoolman, but he also had no time for the humanists and those who sought to recover classical learning. He was not a 'renaissance man'!

Luther's call for reformation was triggered by something which had become much more pressing. He was incensed by increases in the sale of Indulgencies and the corruption at the heart of this scheme to raise money for the rebuilding of St Peters' in Rome.

> The Indulgence he believed to be pernicious because it was misleading simple souls. He saw it as an external and damnable symptom of so much that was inwardly wrong with the Christian teaching of his generation, a teaching which asserted or suggested that God could be placated by external acts, by forms, by payments, by good works (Chadwick, 1964:46).

Luther could no longer tolerate the way in which the Church was abusing its power and set out to challenge the authority of the Pope on this and a whole host of other issues. He preached a return to a simpler faith unencumbered by the trappings of ecclesiastical power. He called for the authority of the Bible to replace the authority of the Church.

Calvin was a generation later than Luther, and as Chadwick puts it, 'The problem now was not the overthrow of the papacy, but the construction of new modes of power'. Luther had preached about the priesthood of all believers and applied it within the Lutheran Church. Calvin, however, argued that 'what was required was a rightly called and purified ministry'. He goes on,

> In breaking down papal authority, the Reformation seemed to have left the authority of the Christian ministry vague and uncertain. Where authority existed among the Protestant Churches, apart from the personal authority of individual men of stature, it rested with the prince or the city magistrate. Calvin believed that in organising the Church at Geneva he must organise it in imitation of the primitive Church, and thereby reassert the independence of the Church and the divine authority of its ministers (Chadwick, 1964:83).

That was the European Reformation. The situation in England was very different. As David Edwards writes in *Christian England*:

> For almost a thousand years it had been Christian England, a people not entirely holy or moral but taking pride in its saints and monasteries, a scene of honour for the clergy and of genuine devotion among many of the laity. Although there had been some rebels there had been more pilgrims and many more conformists right up to the sudden storm of the Reformation in the 1530s (Edwards, 1989:23).

This was at first a political revolution triggered by the determination of Henry VIII to marry Anne Boleyn and his subsequent break with Rome. However, it turned into a religious revolution as successively the Catholic and Protestant causes were taken up by those with power in the land. The vigorous persecution of their respective opponents simply increased the tension. In Edward VI's reign it was Protestantism that prevailed; in Mary's reign Roman Catholicism was restored. In the reign of Elizabeth I, however, the pendulum began to settle in the middle ground and the Church of England was born. The success of this enterprise had much to do with the ability, character and longevity of the reign of Elizabeth. Cranmer's *Book of Common Prayer* also played an important role in giving the new Church its identity.

At the heart of the English Reformation was a clash of authority. For Catholics, God revealed himself primarily through the history, traditions and teachings of the Church with the Pope at its head. For Protestants, scripture was the primary, and for some the only, means of revelation. For the Church of England, the middle way implied a recognition of the part played by both scripture and tradition but it went further than this. Richard Hooker (1553-1600), who is credited with formulating the distinctive Church of England 'take' on authority embraced both scripture and tradition, together with reason, as ways in which God's authority is mediated, argued for a fresh understanding of these elements and the relationship between them.

Despite the progress of reformation in England, there were still those who sought to frustrate the establishment of the new church. There were still significant numbers of Roman Catholics who refused to attend services. These recusants found priests prepared to flout the new regulations and to celebrate mass in secret. They were supported by Catholics from abroad and given particular encouragement by the Jesuits. The pressure on these recusants increased during the reign of Elizabeth but their numbers were such that they never posed a significant threat except in the North of England where opposition was swiftly extinguished. Of considerably more significance was the threat from the Puritans.

Although, a number of different groups were described as Puritans, 'the puritan idea may be found at its most distinctive and coherent and authentic among the Calvinists' (Chadwick, 1964:175-176). For these groups, reformation had not gone far enough. They wanted the removal of crosses in churches and everything that detracted from the simplicity of worship. They wanted the Bible to be at the centre of church life and the Prayer Book to be rooted in it. They believed in predestination and so for them there was a clear division between the 'sheep' and the 'goats'. They believed in austerity and discipline. They had a strong moral sense.

Elizabeth sought compromise between the extremes of Catholicism and Protestantism and wished to establish a distinctive Church of England. But there was opposition to this 'middle way' both from Puritans and from Recusants. Furthermore, it was not yet clear what form this 'middle way' might take since the 'new' church was far from secure and many of its leaders were weak and ineffectual. Arguments focussed on the question of authority, with the Puritans demanding scriptural warrant for every aspect of faith and practice, and the Episcopalians claiming that changes taking place did not conflict with that authority. The Puritans were very effective in spreading their message.

During the reigns of the Stuart kings the country remained enthusiastically and authentically religious, and both James and Charles had firm religious convictions. However, they were inept politicians and had no coherent policy for dealing with divisions within the church. In particular, they seriously underestimated the threat from the Puritans. Both men were obsessed with their own self-importance and with what they believed to be their God-given right to rule. Charles claimed the 'divine right of kings' in principle and pursued policies of 'divide and rule' in practice. The separation between king and country increased and a clash was inevitable.

The Civil War which erupted in 1642 was not a religious war but a battle between King and Parliament. However, the battle between the two wings of the Church was caught up in this wider conflict and divisions widened as a result. Yet despite the inclination of Oliver Cromwell towards Puritanism, he presided over a regime that was remarkably tolerant. On Cromwell's death there was a power vacuum and it soon became clear that only a restoration of the monarchy would restore stability. Although the Puritans were the losers in the conflict, and the Episcopalians the winners, it was some time before the establishment of the Church of England was secure.

The Age of Reason

Following the restoration of the monarchy, Puritanism became Dissent and along with other dissenting groups it suffered persecution. Those who refused to swear allegiance to the king or participate in the rites of the Church of England were branded as traitors and punished or at least denied public office. Various Acts of Parliament were passed restricting the activities of the various groups and their ministers but the futility of all this eventually dawned on the king and in 1689 the Act of Toleration was passed. Thereafter Dissenters were free to practice their faith but they did not always thrive because they were still considered 'second-class citizens'. Moreover, persecution had caused lasting damage to the whole movement – 'by crippling leadership, by narrowing its appeal to society and by destroying the Presbyterian synods'. On the basis of a survey carried out in the early years of the following century it has been estimated that, 'those attending Dissenting places of worship then amounted to just over six per cent of the population of almost 5,500,000, nearly 180,000 of them being Presbyterians, nearly 60,000

Independents, nearly 60,000 Baptists and nearly 40,000 Quakers'. Although a perceived strength of these congregations was the way in which they were governed by the 'church meeting' of members, in practice groups often had to submit to powerful groups of pew-holders, subscribers and trustees. As the years passed, numbers fell and many of these forms of non-conformity declined. Many Presbyterians became Unitarians, a more radical group which rejected the Doctrine of the Trinity. Independents who remained loyal to Calvinism were at the forefront of the forthcoming evangelical revival. Of all the dissenting groups, only the Quakers survived intact (Edwards, 1989:444).

Following the turbulence of the Civil Wars, and despite strong feelings and resentment on all sides, there was a longing amongst many for a quieter life and a simpler faith. The Quakers, or The Society of Friends as they came to be known, called for a return to the simplicity of Christ's teaching and its impact on the individual conscience. They rejected the outward signs of religion and embraced the notion of an 'inner light'. The movement survived because it gained respect amongst large sections of the population for the integrity of its members. It also had a tight organisation and strong leadership. The same could not be said for other dissenting groups nor for the Catholic and Protestant wings of the established church. G M Trevelyan writes of the Quakers:

To maintain the Christian quality in the world of business and of domestic life, and to maintain it without pretensions or hypocrisy, was the great achievement of these extraordinary people… The Puritan pot had boiled over, with much heat and fury; when it had cooled and been poured away, this precious sediment was left at the bottom (Edwards, 1989:355).

1660 was an important year, not only for the restoration of the monarchy, but also for founding of The Royal Society.

Fundamental changes were also taking place in the intellectual climate with the emergence of modern science. The medieval mind had been dominated by superstition, and a blurring of distinctions between religion, magic and science. The world of modern science was to be a very different place but the transition took time. It was not until 1685 that the execution of 'witches' came to an end. At the same time, Newton was still dabbling in alchemy. As the population eventually lost confidence in magic, there was perhaps a danger that religion might suffer the same fate. This did not happen because the pioneers of science firmly rejected magic but had no quarrel with religious faith. They saw the worlds of science and religion as different manifestations of the same creator God. The pioneers of the new 'rational theology', like the 'Cambridge Platonists', appealed to the Bible but interpreted it in the light of reason and conscience. They rejected the claim that in interpreting the Bible for themselves, educated individuals would destroy the power of the Gospel. They believed that the indwelling of God in the mind enabled right interpretation. Edwards describes this new theology as 'no shallow rationalism' but as 'a kind of Quakerism for sober and educated Church of England people'. He goes on:

> The work of the theologians who pioneered in this way deserves to be remembered, for it was courageous work. In the whole history of Christianity, there had been no exact precedent for this attempt to reconcile religion and reason (Edwards, 1989:366).

The period between the restoration of Charles II in 1660 and the flight of James II in 1688 was a very unsettled period despite the wish of many for a quieter life. Charles II was found to be a weak, vacillating and self-indulgent king who became less and less tolerant as his reign progressed. He appeared to have no firm religious convictions but converted on his deathbed. James

II was a proud and arrogant man who had little time for the welfare of his subjects. But he was more genuinely religious than his father and converted to Roman Catholicism. He was attracted to Roman Catholicism because it claimed more authority than the Church of England, and seemed to support his notion of the 'divine right of kings'. He was an unpopular king both with his subjects and his ministers. When opposition to his reign increased, and when the birth of a son increased the threat of a wholesale return to Roman Catholicism, he fled the country.

With the 'glorious revolution' and the accession of William and Mary in 1689 the country entered a prolonged period of relative stability, but one which was still strongly influenced by the particular allegiances of the sovereign. William came from a Calvinistic background and was more sympathetic to the Dissenters. Mary was an Anglican but obeyed her husband as her religion taught her. Anne, who became Queen in 1702, was a strong supporter of the 'high church' and conservative wing of the Church of England. Dissenters were again under pressure. Although George I and George II, reigning from 1714 and 1727 respectively, went through the motions of support, they showed little real commitment to the church, and their reigns are characterised by a period of stagnation and decline. As opposition to the established church decreased, its leaders and people became complacent. Leadership failed and standards dropped. The first half of the eighteenth century was a low point for the spiritual life of the country. The Church of England needed a transfusion of new blood and new ideas.

Fortunately, changes were taking place that would revolutionise both country and church. When George III ascended the throne in 1760, the population was increasing fast and the country was growing in strength as a nation. The Church of England was well established and thriving in many parishes. But the world was changing fast. The American Declaration of Independence in 1776 was a shock to the system and the French

Revolution in 1789 caused reverberations throughout Europe. In Britain people began to question the old social order and the aspirations of an enlarged population needed to be addressed.

> Reason, decorum and elegance had been admired as the cultural equivalents of the political stability which had been such a relief after the turmoil of the seventeenth century. Now the sunny afternoon was over and the climate of opinion was stormy. A new restlessness and a new individualism emerged... (and) gradually the new stirring became the nineteenth's century's faith in intuition, emotion, energy and heroism... It became a cultural revolution, to be called Romanticism (Edwards, 1989:15).

This new emotional energy was the key to what became known as the Evangelical Revival. It started with The Great Awakening in America in the 1730s where the emotional power of the preaching of Jonathan Edwards and others breathed new life into Calvinism. This more 'warm hearted' religion revitalised the mainstream but inevitably polarised opinion on the fringes. At one extreme were those who dismissed these new enthusiasms as no more than irrational outbursts which were no worthy of serious attention. At the other, were those who took the opportunity of this emotionally charged religion to exploit the guilt and fear of the more vulnerable members of society. George Whitfield preached widely in both countries, but it is John Wesley who is more closely identified with the Evangelical Revival in Britain. They were not close for had very different theological views and were very different personalities. Whitfield was a Calvinist but Wesley could not accept the doctrine of predestination and inclined towards Arminianism. Whitfield was the better preacher, but Wesley was the better organiser. The Methodist Church is Wesley's lasting memorial although he would have regretted its formal separation from the

Church of England which became inevitable after his death.

The impact of this revival was also felt in society at large as evangelicals of wealth and influence made their mark. The Clapham Sect brought together a group of such men who were dedicated to the reform of working conditions and other social inequalities. William Wilberforce was a member of the group and led the ultimately successful campaign to abolish slavery. From his first speech against the slave trade in the House of Commons in 1787 to the emancipation of the slaves just before his death in 1833 he worked tirelessly for the cause. But evangelicals like Wilberforce not only sought to change the moral fabric of society. They also sought to spread the Christian message to the wider world. In speech of 1813 he said, 'Christianity assumes her true character... when she takes under protection those poor degraded beings on whom philosophy looks down with disdain' (Edwards, 1989:94).

Although the evangelical revival arose from within the Church of England, the impact of this movement on the established church was limited. Some good work was taking place in the parishes, but overall it remained a conservative institution with a huge investment in social stability and the status quo. It suffered from absent priests and poor attendance and was in need of serious reform. In the event this reform did not come from the top echelons of the church but from laymen who saw the need for change both within the church itself and in its relation to the population at large. On the one hand, there were initiatives to improve the governance of the church and its financial management, and an increase in church building to cope with a rising population. On the other hand, the education of the poor began to be taken seriously in the foundation of the National Society in 1811, and the missionary enterprise in India was expanded. New men gave the Church of England new vigour.

Dissenters were, however, invigorated by the evangelical

revival and the movement later known as Nonconformity became a powerful force in nineteenth century England with as many as one third of the population identified with it. Individual churches were given a new tease of life and denominations embarked on ambitious projects. The Baptist Missionary Society was founded in 1792 closely followed by The London Missionary Society in 1795. The Sunday School movement which opened its first school in 1831 was the only form of education that some poor children received. Despite this enthusiasm, the Dissenters were not all of one mind theologically and tensions arose particularly between orthodox believers and those who denied the doctrine of the Trinity. The Unitarian Society was founded in 1791 and attracted significant numbers of the middle classes.

The Methodists themselves suffered serious schism following the death of John Wesley as different groups interpreted his legacy in different ways. Disagreements centered on the way the movement should be governed and on the way it should undertake its task. The conservative Wesleyan Methodists wanted a hierarchical form of government and no involvement in politics. The breakaway Methodist New Connexion rebels wanted a more democratic structure with ministers regarded as 'servants' and not 'masters'. In due course other groups parted company with the mainstream. Officially, all groups were against involvement in politics but some individual members of breakaway groups defied such guidelines. In due course most groups were reunited.

Roman Catholics remained a persecuted minority throughout this period. There was a residual fear of a wholesale return to Catholicism in England, and a deep rooted prejudice against Catholics particularly in Ireland. Catholic emancipation was granted in 1829 in the face of threats of disorder from Ireland, and large numbers immigrated into England in the face of the potato famines of 1845-47. This influx caused problems not only because the numbers were difficult to accommodate with limited numbers of priests, but also because Irish Catholicism was very distinctive. Irish Catholics needed priests who could appeal to the raw and dramatic forms of liturgy and worship with which they were more familiar than the rather conservative and sober piety of English Catholicism. Priests from the continent largely fulfilled this need.

It is worth pausing at this point to note that alongside, what Edwards describes as, 'these rich formative years' for English Christianity, there were other changes which, though 'harder to pin down' were significant 'movements of thought about man and God' (Edwards, 1989:131). An important part of this shift was the reaction against the Enlightenment which we call Romanticism. It was an appeal to passion and imagination in contrast to reason and intellect, and is well illustrated in the life and work of three poets – William Blake, William Wordsworth and Samuel Taylor Coleridge. Blake was a visionary and mystic who rebelled against authority in both church and state. Wordsworth was not a thinker but a feeler and sought out the spiritual in everyday people and events and led him close to pantheism. Coleridge was more a thinker and sought a spiritual basis for belief which also led him beyond the boundaries of orthodox Christian belief. His legacy is a call for religion to be at the centre of life.

The Victorian Church

Owen Chadwick introduces his two volume study of *The Victorian Church* with these words:

> Victorian England was religious. Its churches thrived and multiplied, its best minds brooded over divine metaphysic and argued about moral principle, its authors and painters and architects and poets seldom forgot that art and literature shadowed eternal truth or beauty, its legislators professed outward and often accepted inward allegiance to divine law,

its men of empire ascribed national greatness to the providence of God and Protestant faith. The Victorians changed the face of the world because they were assured. Untroubled by doubt whether Europe's civilisation and politics were suited to Africa or Asia, they saw vast opportunities open to energy and enterprise, and identified progress with the spread of English intelligence and English industry. They confidently used the word English to describe Scots and Welsh and Irish. Part of their confidence was money, a people of increasing wealth and prosperity, an ocean of retreating horizons. And part was of the soul. God is; and we are his servants, and under his care, and we will do our duty' (Chadwick, 1971:1).

Despite this air of confidence, there were severe challenges ahead. The Roman Catholics needed to be emancipated for the Irish represented a large proportion of the population. The Dissenters needed to be freed from discrimination and to be given equality before the law. There were constant cries for disestablishment as conservative and reactionary leaders of the Church of England continued to stifle reform both in the church and in the social and political worlds. But reform in both church and state there had to be if social unrest was to be avoided and demands for disestablishment dissipated. Popular resentment against compulsory tithes to support the clergy and rates to support the church had to be addressed. In the event it was Robert Peel and the Ecclesiastical Commissioners who came to the rescue. Backed by parliament, they carried out extensive reforms despite opposition from vested interests. Bishops in particular had enjoyed considerable power and were loath to lose it.

The evangelical movement in England was boosted by a second evangelical awakening in the USA which began in 1857, and which reached England soon afterwards through the efforts of people like Dwight Moody. The first Keswick Convention in

1875 and The Cambridge Intercollegiate Christian Union founded in 1877 are among the many evangelical institutions which arose at this time and survive to this day. But the movement had a rather narrow and dated theology and supporters were forced on the defensive by a series of massive movements over which they had no control. The gathering pace of biblical criticism, the rise of The Oxford Movement and the publication of *The Origin of Species* all challenged their convictions about biblical authority and reformation theology. However, this did not diminish the real strength of the evangelical movement in the nineteenth century which continued to be in pastoral work and in social reform. These efforts were pioneered not only by a small number of prominent men like Lord Shaftesbury, but also by many others who lacked that kind of distinction. It is partly as a result of their relative obscurity that the achievements of these men made less impact than those of The Oxford Movement.

The Oxford Movement was a drive for renewal in the Catholic tradition of the Church of England and was led by prominent churchmen – John Keble, Edward Pusey and John Henry Newman among them. The movement started as a reaction against government attempts at the reform of the church in Ireland but became a major force within the established church throughout the land. The start of the movement is usually associated with a sermon by John Keble in St Mary's Church, Oxford in 1833 in which he warned of 'national apostasy'. The aims of the subsequent movement were to instil a greater holiness and vigour in a wing of the church that had not unfairly been dubbed the 'high and dry' tradition. There was a new emphasis on the sacraments, on episcopy, and on the church as the body of Christ. Ordinances for directing and disciplining members were given more respect, decoration and visual enhancement of churches was encouraged, and the ancient traditions of the church were given new weight. It was a movement which had considerable impact both on the Church of England and on the Roman Catholic Church.

Chartism has been described as 'the first great working-class political movement in the history of the world' (Edwards, 1989:194). It was a movement of anger and frustration at the failure of the government to enfranchise all adult members of the population, and to reform parliament and the way members were elected. It was also directed at issues of poverty and exploitation of the poor. It takes its name from the 'People's Charter' which listed the principal aims of the movement. Charles Kingsley described himself as a Chartist, but there were others like F.D. Maurice who opposed the political aims of the Chartists but who supported the need for social reform. Such men were amongst the founders of Christian Socialism which was active in social reform in the mid nineteenth century. Although initiated by members of the Church of England it did not receive wholehearted support from the wider church and declined as a movement though it influence continued to be felt and its work marked the beginning of the modern social movement in the Church of England.

In the second half of the nineteenth century there was a revival in the fortunes of the Church of England. The number and morale of the clergy increased, new churches were built and old churches took on a new lease of life, attendance at services increased and the singing of hymns became more widespread. Leadership improved as able men with proven track records like Samuel Wilberforce were appointed as bishops. Leaders also emerged from the ranks of layman in the church with William Gladstone an important example. His Christian principles were at the heart of his work as a politician and he believed passionately that there can be no separation between religion and politics. His moral principles are best illustrated by his work for the Reform Bill in England and the Home Rule Bill in Ireland. He made mistakes but he was a man of principle.

The Nonconformist movement also gained in strength during the nineteenth century, not only as a religious movement but also with an interest in political and social reform. It fought against the privileges enjoyed by the established church, and struggled unsuccessfully for disestablishment of the Church of England and against the monopoly in education. At times it was associated with particular political groupings but had no coherent strategy and lacked the necessary resources to achieve political ends. It was much more successful in social reform and as migration to the cities increased it offered support particularly to the working class. Temperance campaigns were mounted to deal with the problem of alcohol abuse. In moral and religious matters their strength was in preaching and important centres were established in the major cities.

Victorian religion was not only challenged by political, social and economic issues but also by intellectual, scientific and cultural movements. The faith of many Victorians was based on theological and doctrinal foundations which had not changed much since the Reformation. Political and social issues were being informed by new understandings of how Christianity should work in practice. Intellectual and cultural movements now also needed to be informed by fresh approaches if uncertainty, scepticism and even contempt for religion were to be tackled. In particular, the reactionary, dogmatic and authoritarian aspects of the old religion needed to be reformed at a time when people were beginning to think for themselves. It is no coincidence that by the end of the nineteenth century, secularism was well established and with it the foundation of the National Secular Society in 1866 and the Rationalist Press Association in 1899. There were increasing numbers of people who simply did not believe in the old certainties.

This movement of secularisation is well illustrated by the attitude of Charles Darwin as he realised the implications of his scientific discoveries. Edwards describes how during his voyage on HMS *Beagle* (1831-1836) he 'lost the complacent Christianity which he had imbibed from the *Evidences* of William Paley' as he contemplated the real world which was opening up before his eyes. He goes on to explain that Darwin's *Origin of Species* (1859).

> ...was sensational not because it propounded a complete explanation of the evolution of man from lower animals, but because men who had open eyes concluded that the Bible could not be literally true in its accounts of creation – and became inclined to suspect that the Bible was not true in any sense... It is curious that in England the main challenge to the old authority of revelation came from the new science, whereas in Germany much more interest was taken in detailed historical criticism of the Old and New Testaments' (Edwards, 1989:296).

The Twentieth Century

At the start of the twentieth century the Church of England was the 'established' church but it never had been and never would be a 'national' church. It was not just that there were significant numbers of Roman Catholics and Free Churchmen practising their faith in very different ways, but that the membership and complexion of the Church of England clearly distinguished it from these other groups. Although generalisations can be misleading, it would not be too far from the mark to state that large numbers of its members were politically Conservative, were from the higher socio-economic classes, saw themselves as part of an educated elite and were 'high' in their churchmanship. Many were also temperamentally conservative, socially class-conscious and sometimes personally aloof. They liked to think of themselves as 'Christian gentleman', a term used by Thomas Arnold, headmaster of Rugby School from 1828 to 1842, to describe his aspirations for his pupils.

In his contribution to The Year Book of Education 1961

entitled *'The Gentlemen': the Evolution of an English Ideal*, Edmund King writes,

> The 'gentleman' ideal combines at least two of the following ingredients: the feudal knight, a servant as he himself is served; the Christian knight-errant, constrained by personal honour in subjection to a divine master, and giving aid to the unfortunate; the troubadour, with his romantic and unconsummated love-ideal; the pilgrim, especially in Bunyan's sense, but not excluding the self-righteous self-sufficiency of Robinson Crusoe; the post-Renaissance humanist; and the 'civilised and civilising' Conquistador. Formidable though this composite picture is, it still omits the most important feature of corporate loyalty to one's peer group' (Bereday, 1961).

Most of those in the upper echelons of the Church of England and many of those in the pews were products of the Public School system and saw themselves as 'Public School Men'. The qualities of character that have been associated with this label have been expressed in a number of ways, but included manliness, toughness and 'standing on one's own feet'. They also included self-confidence and the ability to be at ease, not just with their peers but with all sections of society. They included modesty, respect and consideration for others. They included the notion of 'fair play'. Good manners were taken for granted. These qualities put these men in a strong position to take their place both in the city clubs and regimental mess, and in the working world as leaders in their various fields. These qualities were also regarded as prerequisites for service in the British Empire.

Bernard Darwin, in *The English Public School*, published in 1929, describes public schoolboys as follows:

> Many a lad, who leaves an English Public School disgracefully

ignorant of the rudiments of useful knowledge, who can speak no language but his own, and writes that imperfectly, to whom the noble literature of his country and the stirring history of his forefathers are almost a sealed book, and who has devoted a great part of his time and nearly all his thoughts to athletic sports, yet brings away with him something beyond all price, a manly, straightforward character, a scorn of lying and meanness, habits of obedience and command, and fearless courage. Thus equipped, he goes out into the world, and bears a man's part in subduing the earth, ruling its wild folk, and building up the Empire; doing many things so well that it seems a thousand pities that he was not trained to do them better, and to face the problems of race, creed and government in distant corners of the Empire with a more instructed mind. This type of citizen, however, with all his defects, has done yeoman's service to the Empire; and for much that is best in him our public schools may fairly take credit' (Darwin, 1929:21).

In his essay, Darwin implies that the nature of the education received in these schools had both positive and negative impacts on the subsequent careers of those who attended them. On the positive side, the emphasis on quality of character did produce people who had those qualities that enabled them to take an active role in society and to lead. With leadership comes a willingness to take responsibility and to set an example, qualities that were firmly established in the public schools and in the people who taught in them. On the other hand, the negative impact of public school life was that too often the qualities of character that former pupils possessed obscured other less desirable qualities. Those with these very worthy qualities of character were often strong personalities who were inclined to speak their minds. They too often displayed prejudiced, arrogant and ignorant assumptions about the world outside their immediate experience.

Those in the upper echelons of society and who had been nurtured in this particular way often displayed particularly narrow and inflexible attitudes in the authority that they exercised in their professional life. They also expected those 'below' them to follow their lead. This was certainly true in the Armed Services but it was also true in the Christian Church. It is understandable that military personnel must obey orders without question from senior officers in the interests of good order and discipline. It is perhaps less obvious that clergy should obey bishops in the same way yet many bishops expected allegiance of this kind. Although some nurtured their clergy more sympathetically, others simply carried over their experience of military command to the quite different world of the Christian Church. There had always been those who exercised authority in this particular way but the ethos of the Public Schools encouraged the view that obedience to authority was a virtue in its own right.

The Ecumenical Scene

With the rise of the ecumenical movement in the twentieth century, and as a direct result of the meeting between Pope Paul VI and Archbishop Michael Ramsey in 1966, an Anglican/Roman Catholic Joint Preparatory Commission was established and met for the first time in 1967. In *The Malta Report* of 1968, the Commission identified a number of areas of agreement between the two Churches. They also noted specific areas of disagreement and the Anglican Roman Catholic International Commission proposed by the Report was recommended to:

> ...undertake two urgent and important tasks: one, to examine the question of intercommunion, and the related matters of Church and Ministry and, the other, to examine the question of authority, its nature, exercise, and implications' (Anglican/

Roman Catholic Joint Preparatory Commission 1968).

In their first report, members of the Commission noted the achievement of 'a consensus on authority in the Church and, in particular, on the basic principles of primacy'. However, when they moved from basic principles to 'particular claims of papal primacy and to its exercise', problems arose. These problems were, the weight given to biblical texts about Peter's authority, the meaning of the 'divine right' of the successors of Peter, the affirmation of papal infallibility, and the nature of the jurisdiction ascribed to the bishop of Rome as universal primate (Anglican/Roman Catholic Joint Preparatory Commission 1976).

Unpacking the Gift, edited by Peter Fisher, is a series of reflections on the document, *The Gift of Authority,* published by the Commission. In one essay, Martyn Percy writes:

> The centre of Anglicanism is seldom found in doctrine, but rather, the manner in which that doctrine is held' (Fisher, 2002:83).

Paul Avis was prompted to write at length in response to the Final Report of ARCIC with which he had fundamental disagreements. In, *Ecumenical Theology and the Elusiveness of Doctrine,* he writes:

> Interpreters of Anglicanism are sometimes compelled to resort to an appeal to its spirit or 'ethos'. This necessity is often regarded as the Achilles heel of Anglicanism, especially by those – Anglicans or Roman Catholics as the case may be – who require a cut-and-dried propositional statement of Christian truth. But to those who hold to a 'personalist' understanding of truth as a reality that is open to discovery through praxis rather than theory, through Christian life and liturgy, it is certainly not something to be defensive about...

Fundamental differences there are – but the *insuperable* ones are not of a doctrinal nature. They are differences of 'horizon', of ultimate assumptions regarding the approach to truth and the methods, norms and sources of theology (Avis, 1986:x-xii).

For Avis, the problem with the ARCIC discussions is that they have 'apparently been confined to purely doctrinal matters'. For him, doctrinal matters cannot be successfully tackled unless ' the ground has been prepared by thrashing out a common approach to the most basic assumptions of our theology'. This would include discussion of 'modern theological *method*; the nature of *revelation*; the character of *truth* and the logical and linguistic status of *doctrines.*

The root of the problem seems to be that the Anglican members of ARCIC have been willing to go along with a concept of truth (and error) that is deeply entrenched in the Roman Catholic tradition, but profoundly inimical to the ethos of Anglicanism. It is the difference between a *propositional* (or analytical) and a *personal* (or fiduciary) understanding of the nature of truth (Avis, 1986:7).

This problem persists and it remains to be seen whether Pope Francis will shift the emphasis in the course of his pontificate. In the meantime issues of power and authority remain unresolved in the Roman Catholic Church and are at least a contributing factor in the scandal of child abuse in Ireland.

The sexual abuse of children in Ireland

A leading article in *The Tablet* of 30 May 2009 comments on the publication of the Ryan Commission Report on the abuse of children in Ireland:

Catholic Ireland has suffered a series of moral earthquakes

that have shaken it to its foundations. The latest shock arises from the publication of the Ryan Commission Report into the industrial school system that used to be run by religious orders, where appalling cruelty was endemic and institution-alised. Other reports are expected this summer into sexual abuse committed by priests and the efforts by church author-ities to cover it up.

The article continues:

It is clear that the problem was not just 'a few bad apples' or even a whole barrel of them, but the arrogance of an almighty Church too powerful for its own good. It is useless to blame the state or society for allowing it to happen. The blame lies within the Church itself. The power and the glory that were so badly misused had a theological, even ideological, basis. This told the Church that it was 'a true and perfect society' (in the words of Pius 1X): whatever it did was right, and whatever might contradict that impression had to be suppressed (The Tablet, 2009).

Sadly, of course, the abuse of children in Ireland is only part of a much more widespread pattern of abuse in religious institutions throughout the world. And it will be many years before the full extent of that abuse is revealed as investigations are undertaken and reports are commissioned. As the article recognises, the scandal is not only that abuse took place but that it was concealed by the authorities. And the abuse of power is at the heart of the problem.

One of the underlying causes of this abuse of power is the clericalism that has been and still is a particular feature of Irish Catholicism. Clericalism arises when the ordained clergy are given excessive deference by the people and when they exceed their influence over the people in matters both inside and outside the church. In an article in the journal *Pastoral Psychology* entitled, *Roman Catholic Clericalism, Religious Duress and Clergy Sexual Abuse*, Thomas P Doyle writes:

> Clericalism has deluded Church members and non-members alike into thinking that deference to the clergy is both a sign of faith in God and an act pleasing to God. In truth, clericalism with all its unpleasant manifestations, *uses* the good faith of individuals to manipulate and exploit them. The victim and family who fail to call attention to sexual abuse by a cleric, or the judge who allows a guilty priest abuser to get off lightly, or who massages the judicial system to prevent a diocese from being sued for civil damages, responds to clericalism's manipulative power but not to an authentic respect for God (Doyle, 2003).

Doyle comments that 'clergy sexual abuse cases are complex phenomena' but identifies some common features:

> The actual sexual abuse itself is the most visible and dramatic aspect of the case, but is far from the whole story. Sexual abuse by the clergy is not something isolated from the dynamics of Church power structures. Clericalist control and traumatic bonding are the most important aspects in cases of abuse perpetrated by the clergy. These two human dynamics explain why the clergy are able to seduce people and subject them to a pattern of debilitating sexual abuse (Doyle, 2003).

'Traumatic bonding' occurs when cycles of reward and punishment creates powerful emotional bonds that are resistant to change. This points towards the psychological damage that can be caused by abuse and the lasting harm that the victims can suffer.

Conclusion

Power is a real problem. Although it is not possible to exercise authority without power, the old saying that 'power corrupts and absolute power corrupts absolutely', attributed to Lord Acton in 1887, is a warning to us all.

The 'crisis of authority' in the Christian Church

The year that changed history

The Guardian describes 1968 as 'the year that changed history':

> It was a year of seismic social and political change across the globe. From the burgeoning anti-Vietnam war and civil rights movements in the United States, protests and revolutions in Europe and the first comprehensive coverage of war and resultant famine in Africa. The world would never be the same again (http://www.theguardian.com/observer/gallery/2008/jan/17/1).

In 1968 I was on holiday in the United States and was in Chicago at the time of the Democratic Convention. The convention was being held against a background of violence, political and civil unrest, and riots in many cities following the assassinations of Martin Luther King and Robert F. Kennedy earlier in the year. The convention was electing a prospective presidential candidate and Kennedy had been one of the contenders. The tension was palpable.

But it was not just in the United States that authority was being challenged and usurped. The Warsaw Pact invasion of Czechoslovakia halted the political reforms of Alexander Dubček's Prague Spring. There was widespread civil unrest in France and a general strikes as well as the occupation of universities and factories across the country. In Nigeria, the Civil War continued to cause havoc as rival ethnic groups sought to gain power. In Britain, racial tensions were raised by Enoch Powell's 'rivers of blood' speech.

If

1968 was also the year in which the film *If* was released. Some scenes were filmed at Aldenham School where I spent the bulk of my professional career. A number of the pupils took part and the Headmaster, Paul Griffin, wrote about it as follows:

In about 1967, I had a visit from Lindsay Anderson who wanted to make a film about a public school. We needed the money but I was cautious. I asked to see the script that eventually arrived. It seemed very short for a full-length film, but innocuous enough. Nothing like what eventually emerged could have passed my scrutiny, only a suggestion that at this or that point a character would have daydreams but I could have no suspicion as to what they could be. As it was, I gave maximum assistance to Anderson in making one of the most brilliant and destructive films ever produced – *If...* The public schools were, in complete disregard of Anderson's assurance, mercilessly and hilariously sent up (Edwards and Wood, 1997:112).

If was certainly a highly controversial film and, as there was no clear line between fantasy and reality in the film, there was much debate about what it was actually about. On the face of it, the film is an allegorical story of pupil rebellion in an old established public school. For some, it was clearly an attack on the public school system. For others, the use of public school images was simply a means to an end. In conversation with Paul Griffin many years later, I was clear that, for him, Anderson was attacking the establishment of which the public schools were a major part. The following review appeared in *The Listener* at the time:

In last summer's *Sight and Sound* David Robinson wrote of *If...* 'Above all, the film is not intended to be about public

79

schools, a realistic study of the educational system. Anderson sees it as an epic intention, "a metaphor, if you like, of life in Britain today – the image of the school as a reflection of a certain British tradition or if you like of a hierarchical society...'" I think that these intentions should have been made clearer in the film. Most people seeing it will think that, though its often grotesque and fantastical style demarcates it clearly from documentary, its accumulation of realistic detail and its use of certain public school stereotypes do inevitably build up into an indictment of the public school system (Rhode, 1968).

Whatever the impressions of the film were elsewhere, the impact on the boys at Aldenham School was considerable, and the film provided, what Paul Griffin describes as, a 'powerful focus' for much of the unrest during that decade:

If made 1968 the low point of our time at Aldenham. Our boys, seeing themselves in what seemed to them romantic circum-stances, enthusiastically transformed themselves into images of the heroes of the film. It would be stupid to pretend that no other factors entered in but If was a powerful focus. Even the sound boys, of whom there were still plenty, regarded school-masters with a new wariness, while many others looked at our efforts to help and educate with rank hostility... Memories of those days come back to me in flashes – breaking it to individual parents that their sons had smoked cannabis in their own homes; telling a Senior service officer that during the holidays his boy was selling subversive literature in the streets of his home town every Saturday morning... (Edwards and Wood, 1997:112).

1968 was, of course, not the only year in which there was a 'crisis of authority' in the wider world for challenges to authority had been growing for some time but events in that year somehow provided the spark that set the world alight and things were never the same again. But it is the 'crisis of authority' in religious matters that really interests us here.

Humanae Vitae

Of the many religious 'crises' that arose during 1968, the publication of *Humanae Vitae* is perhaps the most significant for it concerned the authority of the Roman Catholic Church and the Pope himself.

Humanae Vitae was an encyclical written by Pope Paul VI and issued on 25 July 1968. Subtitled *On the Regulation of Birth*, it reaffirmed the orthodox teaching of the Roman Catholic Church regarding married love, responsible parenthood, and the continued rejection of most forms of birth control. This last provision was unexpected. The pope had rejected the majority opinion of the Pontifical Commission on Birth Control established by his predecessor on the grounds that any change would have amounted to a discontinuity in teaching. The prohibition on all forms of artificial birth control caused widespread dismay and dissention amongst the faithful.

In August 1968, *The Tablet*, the prominent Roman Catholic weekly publication, staked its reputation with an historic leader under the title, *Crisis in the Church*.

This (the publication of *Humanae Vitae*) will raise, inevitably, questions as to the status of encyclicals, their authority and binding force. Whether they will be devalued or endorsed we cannot predict. A new chapter in the relationship of the Pope with his bishops and with the faithful at large has now opened on a sombre note. There will be doubt and dismay about the Church herself amongst her more reflective members, a new bravado in some sectors: a mutual mistrust. Loyalty to the faith and to the whole principle of authority now consists in this: to speak out about this disillusion of ours, not to be silenced by fear. We who are of the household and can think of no other have the right to question, complain and protest, when conscience impels. We have the right and we have the duty—out of love for the brethren. *Quis nos separabit?* (The Tablet, 1968).

Humanae Vitae was not an *ex cathedra* document and so its contents were not claimed by the pope as an infallible doctrine, but it had papal authority and all members of the church were expected to follow its instructions. In the event, its prohibition on all forms of artificial birth control was widely ignored and caused a crisis of authority in the Catholic Church which continues to this day. The crisis arose because of the disparity between the teaching of the church and the practice of its members. This undermined the authority of the church and continues to do so.

The 'monkey trial'

In the United States it was the authority of the state that was in danger of being undermined in religious matters as the outcome of the 1925 'monkey trial' still reverberated around the country.

Many people in America were reluctant from the start to accept the theory of evolution but by the 1920's, evolution had filtered into the education system. One of the biggest issues was which theory, creationism or evolution, should be taught in schools. Creationism is the notion that God created the world literally as stated in Genesis. The famous 'monkey trial' had a significant impact on views.

In 1925, the state of Tennessee passed a law (the Butler Act) banning the teaching of evolution in favour of creationism in state schools. A young school teacher, John Scopes, tested the law by deliberately teaching evolution, and was brought to court. Although Scopes was found guilty and fined, the case gained considerable publicity and highlighted the issues all over

America. In 1967 the Butler Act was repealed as a result of the trial, and in 1968 the United States Supreme Court prevented any state from banning evolutionary teaching to promote religion. This became an issue of 'freedom of speech' but it did not stop legal challenges which continue to this day.

The background to this debate is the separation of church and state in the United States constitution but the issue here is the different understandings of authority. For those promoting creationism, the Genesis stories are historical accounts of what actually happened. For them the Bible has the authority of literal truth and the words of the Bible are the words of God to be understood literally. For those promoting evolution, the Genesis stories are not about the 'how' of creation but about the 'why'. In other words, these stories are 'myths' which convey religious not scientific truth. For them, evolution was God's chosen method of creation. The stories are therefore still authoritative but in a very different way.

These examples show that the 'crisis of authority' in religious matters was real. We now need to examine how and why they occurred.

'External' and 'internal' authority

In his book, *Voices of Authority*, Nicholas Lash, the Roman Catholic theologian, writes:

> There is in our modern world a widespread crisis in respect of the search for norms, for standards, for direction: in a word, a crisis of authority. The world of today is not only a very different world from that of yesterday, and one that is felt to be very different; it is also a world of unprecedented complexity and of unprecedently rapid and profound change (Lash, 1976:17).

He identifies 'two factors (which) above all have contributed to our contemporary crisis of authority'. He refers to:

> ...first that suspicion of 'external' authority (and, in particular, of the authority of the past) which has characterised Western European modes of thought since the rise of modern science and the enlightenment. Second, the problems posed for the discernment of truth by the bewildering variety of contemporary languages, disciplines, methods and sources of information' (Lash, 1976:1).

This 'crisis of authority' applies to religious authority as much as it does to other aspects of life though there are important distinctions. For Christians, God is their ultimate authority and that authority must be mediated. Traditionally it has been accepted that this authority has been mediated through 'external' sources like scripture, tradition and the church. Increasingly, however, authority has been sought 'internally' through the mediation of reason and experience. Furthermore, not only has there been this shift from 'external' to 'internal' sources of mediation, there has been a shift from a willingness to accept 'external' authentication by others of particular sources to a demand that sources must be 'internally' authenticated by ourselves. The dangers of both aspects of this shift are picked up by Lash:

> If we appeal too exclusively to internal, material criteria of authority, then we shall be in danger of substituting our standards and our experience for the authority of God... if we appeal too exclusively to external, formal criteria of authority, then we shall be implicitly appealing to the authority of a God who is simply alien to human experience' (Lash, 1976:12).

Lash reminds us that 'the notion of authority and the notion of truth are closely related' but that only in God do they become one.

Ultimately, the only authority is the authority of truth: the truth that is God, the source and ground of all truth. The 'problem' of authority, therefore, is the problem of establishing criteria for the discernment and prosecution of truth: for 'hearing' the truth and 'doing' it (Lash, 1976:24).

The 'plurality of voices'.

So the problem of identifying the authentic voice of God is the same as the discernment of ultimate truth. But, despite the unity of God, the human quest for truth is 'irreducibly pluralistic'.

> We employ and we need to employ a rich variety of languages and explanatory frameworks in our efforts to hear the truth and respond to it or, to put it another way, 'God speaks to us in a variety of voices' (Lash, 1976:27).

But that plurality also applies to 'doing' the truth which:

> ...entails recognising a rich variety of 'authorities': church and state, executive and judiciary, teachers and parents, friends and those in need. Or, once again, to put it another way, 'God speaks to us in a variety of decisions and directions' (Lash, 1976:30).

And that plurality of voices is increasing.

> Ever since the renaissance and the development of modern science, the irreducible pluralism of the languages, methods, and criteria of the human quest for truth has been growing increasingly evident, and increasingly complex (Lash, 1976:27).

The difficulties of dealing with this situation are well illustrated with reference to the issue of birth control discussed earlier.

Are there not numerous Christian married couples who, in their attempts honestly and fearlessly to discern the truth, have heard the voices of truth speaking, not simply with different, but with conflicting messages and commands... Are there not numerous Christians who know perfectly well that it is not possible to reconcile... the voices of the anthropological and medical sciences, parental and demographic responsibility, and the official pronouncements of ecclesiastical authority? (Lash, 1976:32).

At the end of the day we all have to make decisions based on a whole range of criteria and it is always a risk that our decisions do not reflect 'the mind of God'.

The normal everyday situation is one in which no single one of the voices of truth speaks to the Christian with uncompromising, absolute authority. The normal everyday situations are such that no single one of the voices of truth may be straightforwardly and exclusively identified with the voice of God; in which no single one of the words that we hear can be declared simply to be, to the exclusion of all others, the 'word of God' (Lash, 1976:32).

The 'plurality of voices' extends to our understanding of the Bible, to our theologies, to our creedal statements and more. Fortunately, there has been a shift amongst individual Christians towards a greater willingness to hear and respond to this pluralism of voices, whether they be from individuals and groups of different traditions, or those who offer insights from different disciplines – anthropology, psychology, sociology and the rest.

Unfortunately, the Church has not always been equally willing to 'hear and respond to the pluralism of voices' and the clergy have not always been prepared to accept the challenge of those who come at things from a different angle. The authority of the church has been seriously compromised by this inability or unwillingness to change.

In his article, *The Psychological Roots of Authority*, published towards the end of a decade of serious challenge to all aspects of authority, Jack Dominian describes the 'crisis of authority' in the church as a 'clamour for change'. He writes:

> This springs from an awareness varying from a deep conviction to a mere glimmer of insight that the Church's authority has been far more concerned with order than with growth, with organisation than with service, with coercion than freedom, with law rather than love (Dominian, 1969).

Jack Dominian expands on this theme in his book, *Authority: A Christian Interpretation of the Psychological Evolution of Authority*. He argues that 'the Christian community as a whole has failed to read the signs of the times accurately and its leaders have made serious errors. The reasons for this failure are threefold':

> The first has been to associate the kingdom of God with an authoritarian system, dependent on the use of authority as a source of power, generating feelings of fear and guilt in its adherents which are foreign to the message of the Christian Gospel, where authority is seen primarily as service.

The second is the failure to discriminate between supporting law and order in the community and the evolution of human relationships from positions which belong to early childhood where inequality, fear and dependency predominate, to the more mature later stages in which maturity is seeking equality of personal worth in the presence of differentiating capacities and characteristics.

The third, and in some ways the most serious, failure of all is that the Christian community has fostered ideals which have encouraged the characteristics of early childhood immaturity, and have perpetuated that immaturity in its various structures, particularly the priesthood (Dominian, 1976:81-82).

There is some hope that there will be change in our understanding of authority because all aspects of church life evolve. Church life cannot stand still, it can only more forwards or backwards. It would not appear to be moving backwards so it must be moving incrementally forward.

The evolution of authority

In the editorial of an issue of *Modern Believing* devoted to articles on 'authority', Martin Percy refers to the book, *Religion and Social Policy*, and Paula Nesbitt's sociological observations on the subject of authority, where she suggests that 'authority has an evolutionary history within any given church or denomination' (Nesbitt, 2001):

She notes that in the first evolutionary phase of denominationalism, or in specific congregational evolution, (which can currently be seen in the early history of new house churches), institutional relations usually can be governed through obedience, and, if necessary, punishment. We might describe this as the exercise of *traditional* authority, where power over another can be nakedly asserted.

However, in the second phase, interpersonal contracts emerge between congregations, regions and individuals. Here 'ecclesial citizenship' is born, and law and order develop into agreed rather than imposed rule. We might call this *rational* authority: it has to be argued for and defended in the face of disputes and questioning. Again, a number of new churches are now at the point where their power and authority need explaining in relation to their context and other relations.

In the third phase (postmodern, etc.), more complex social

contracts emerge between parties, which require a deeper articulation of a shared ethos and an agreement about the nature of a shared moral community. To retain unity and cohesive power, authority must be *negotiated*. It is here that the denomination effectively crosses the bridge from childhood to adulthood. Congregations learn to live with the differences between themselves (or not). Communions or denominations can begin to show signs of strain at this point, not unlike families.

Finally, there is *symbolic* authority. This states that authority and power are constituted in ways of being or dogma that are not easily apprehensible. Networks of congregations may choose a particular office ('chief pastor') or event ('synod') or artefact of tradition ('bible'), and position as having supreme governance. However, the weakness of symbolic authority is often comparable to the dilemma faced by those who prefer monarchical power. By positing power in an office that seldom intervenes in a decisive way, symbolic authority normally has to justify its substance. If it can't, it loses its power and authority. It is at this point that individuals and groups tend to speak up, and pose the question: 'by what authority?'

It is clear that in the contemporary world, all types of authority are going to be subject to penetrating questions. It is also clear that our ability to overcome any 'crisis of authority' will depend on our willingness to answer these questions with intelligence and imagination and to engage in dialogue with patience and flexibility.

What authorities cannot afford to do is remain aloof from dialogue, and merely invest in reassertion and institutional deafness. Good arguments must be reciprocal, and it is only in such contexts that any authority discovers itself to be 'true', rather than merely privileged or dominant (Percy, 2004).

The wider picture

Linda Woodhead is a Professor in the Department of Politics, Philosophy and Religion at Lancaster University, and the organiser of the Westminster Faith Debates. Her research explores the relationship between religious and social change worldwide. In the following article she comments on the contribution of Dr Shuruq Naguib to a debate on the place of religion in the Arab Spring. She writes that Dr Naguib 'left us in no doubt that what's happening is about religion as well as politics and economics. The uprisings coincide with a crisis of religious authority and leadership'.

The issue of authority has become acute for Muslims, but it rumbles not far from the surface in many of the world's religions today, particularly those with a clerical or scholarly class and authoritative texts and tradition. In a democratic age, with vastly increased access to knowledge and learning, why should believers listen to what leaders tell them rather than try to discern the truth for themselves?

It's a question Islam is currently being forced to address, but which all religions will soon have to face. Even in Western democracies, traditional leaderships are in crisis. It's not just that their credentials as the sole legitimate interpreters of religious truth are being questioned by well-informed lay people, it's that they can no longer speak for their "followers."

My recent *YouGov* surveys in Britain found that just 4% of Catholics, 6% of Jewish people and 14% of Muslims now say they take guidance from religious leaders (http://faithdebates.org.uk/research). Even amongst active mosque and church-attenders, that climbs to only 24% of Muslims (the highest for any religion) and 10% of Catholics. Religious leaders still speak but few are listening (Woodhead, 2014).

At least part of the problem arises because governments and those within the public at large without religious associations have not realised that there is an increasing plurality of religious experience amongst those with a religious disposition.

> Far from helping religious institutions to reform, western governments exacerbate the problem. They continue to relate to religion in outdated ways, treating traditional leaders as authoritative representatives of homogenous religious "communities." Meanwhile religion on the ground diversifies and flourishes in new forms and with different actors. What's ignored is the scale and depth of contemporary religious diversity – even within a single religious tradition or institution. And what's fetishized aren't unchanging forms, but a set of 19th and 20th century arrangements which are increasingly out of time (Woodhead, 2014).

It is clear that the crisis of religious authority is not something that will quickly dissipate and will be with us for some time to come. It is also clear that this crisis will change and morph into other forms the shape of which is difficult to predict. We must therefore be open to change so that we are in the best position to handle it.

How do we respond to religious authority?

Introduction

We respond to religious authority in a multitude of different ways and for a multitude of different reasons. In this chapter we shall explore the ways; in the next chapter we shall explore the reasons. We may respond positively, welcome and accept that authority. We may accept that authority with reservations and questions. We may respond negatively and reject it altogether. We may choose to ignore it. Whatever our response, much will depend on the context.

Obedience to a command

The implication of accepting authority is that we will be obedient to that authority, and the extent of that acceptance will be measured by the degree of obedience we are prepared to give. We can illustrate what might be involved in the notion of total obedience by examining the lives of those in religious communities within the Roman Catholic Church. The Society of Jesus (or Jesuits) provide one of the best examples because obedience, along with poverty and chastity, is one of the final vows taken by members of the Society. Furthermore, Ignatius of Loyola, the founder, considered that obedience should be at the heart of the life of the Jesuit. Obedience is therefore an important theme in the foundation documents of the Society (Society of Jesus 1996) and in the correspondence of Ignatius. The various strands of his thought on the matter are brought together in a famous letter of 1553. Ignatius is prompted to write this letter by reports from Portugal that members of the Society are refusing to accept orders from their superiors. This letter sets out his thoughts on the subject of obedience and has become one of the standard formularies of the Society (Ignatius Loyola, 1996).

He begins by stating that, for him, obedience is one of the

highest virtues because 'it is so highly recommended in word and example by Holy Scripture' and because 'as long as obedience is flourishing, all the other virtues will be seen to flourish'. He points out that obedience is not due to superiors because they 'happen to be very good people' but because 'they stand for Him and have His authority'. He goes on to outline the nature of the obedience by explaining that in response to an order from a superior, 'there should be not merely effective execution, but affective agreement' where 'the superior's wishes are made one's own'. But Ignatius goes further:

> Those who set their sights on the complete and perfect offering of themselves to God must not stop at their wishes, but include their thoughts. Not only should there be a single wish, but also a single sense with the superior. We have to subordinate our own judgements to the superior's in so far as it is possible for a judgement to be moved by a pious desire... obedience is nothing less than a holocaust. It is there we can offer ourselves completely, without excluding any part of ourselves, in the fire of love to our Creator and Lord at the hands of His ministers. By obedience one puts aside all that one is, one dispossesses oneself of all that one has, in order to be possessed and governed by divine Providence by means of a superior.

In the same letter, Ignatius shows how obedience brings freedom.

> With great liberality, offer the liberty that He gave you to your Creator and Lord in His ministers. Consider that it is no small privilege of your freedom of will to be able to return it completely in obedience to the One who gave it to you. You do not destroy it in this way; rather you bring it to perfection as you put your own wishes in line with the most sure of all

rightness, the will of God. For you the interpreter of that will is the superior who rules you in the place of God (Ignatius Loyola, 1996:251-260).

At the same time, obedience brings service. In his book, *The Jesuits*, Joseph de Guibert writes:

> In this idea of the servant, too, lies one of the chief reasons for the insistence on total abnegation of self. Abnegation is the virtue proper to the servant; for by definition a servant is not for himself but for his master. This abnegation is the virtue of full and unconditional service. For obedience is the fullest manifestation of this abnegation. Genuine obedience is without anything that is merely passive, basely mercenary, or basely obsequious; but it is intelligent, active, loving, noble, and manly (Guibert, 1964:595).

Although these exhortations seem very severe and uncompromising they were, even in the early years, tempered by humanity and common sense. In his book *The First Jesuits*, John O'Malley writes,

> Nadal (Jeronimo Nadal, 1507-1580) described the general style of obedience and governance in the Society as "sweet and moderate" or, more often, as combining "firmness and sweetness". It was firm in the general goals to be achieved, but mild or sweet in dealing with the individuals concerned, in taking account of their physical and psychological situation by showing patience and moderation toward them and making ample use, when necessary, of *epikeia* and dispensations from general norms' (O'Malley, 1993:354).

And there were exceptions to the rule. Ignatius extols the 'simplicity of blind obedience', but makes clear that 'blind obedience' does not extend to those orders that are sinful or would lead to the commitment of sin. He quotes Bernard of Clairvaux, to the effect that orders from human persons are to be obeyed 'provided of course that the human person gives no order contrary to God' (Ignatius Loyola, 1996:258).

Jesuits in the contemporary world still take the same vows and the notion of obedience remains central to their life and work. However, understandings have changed and under the influence of human sciences there has been a greater awareness of the role of the subject. *The Life of Obedience* was a decree of the Thirty-first General Congregation of the Jesuits in 1966, and was a response to problems arising for the vow of obedience in an increasingly complex world, and stressed the role of the subject in discernment. The decree describes dialogue between superiors and religious as 'funda-mental and essential for the wholesome progress of our Society (Congregation of the Society of Jesus, 1965-1966, 1974-1975).

In commenting on the significance of this decree, Philip Endean SJ writes:

In the last two centuries there have been profound transfor-mations both in our understanding of the human and indeed in the very reality of what it is to be human. The Church's reaction has largely been to resist these changes, and to attempt in ever more futile ways to pretend that they are not occurring. However, although such resistance continues, Vatican II marked the tentative beginning of a more constructive attitude. After the Council, we Jesuits along with the Church as a whole were stimulated to redefine ourselves through a simultaneous looking back on our traditions and looking around at the world in which we find ourselves. The shifts in obedience and discernment are a part of that process (Endean, 1993).

Before these reforms, however, the demand for 'blind obedience' was normative. George Tyrrell (1861-1909) was a Jesuit priest, theologian and scholar. His attempts to evolve and adapt Catholic teaching in the context of the modern world made him a key figure in the Modernist controversy within the Roman Catholic Church in the late 19th century. Tyrrell was disciplined under Pope Pius X and was expelled from the Jesuit order in 1906. In a recent article on Tyrrell in *The Tablet*, Oliver Rafferty writes:

> In one dispute with the superior general, Tyrrell had pointed out that Fr. Martin was wrong as to a number of facts in his case. Fr. Martin took the high-handed view that he, as superior general, had made his will clear to Tyrrell, whose response must be to obey, and if the superior was wrong as to mere matters of fact this was irrelevant in so far as religious obedience was concerned' (Rafferty, 2009:10).

Even in the 1960s, uncompromising demands for 'blind obedience' prevailed. Karen Armstrong has documented her own experience as a Roman Catholic nun in *Through the Narrow Gate*. She was trained before the Second Vatican Council reforms were implemented and so experienced the harsh and uncompromising regime that was not uncommon at the time. The oppressive and stifling atmosphere eventually took its toll and she left the order in considerable physical, mental and spiritual distress. Annie Fox, who was an Anglican nun, points out that the religious life is 'meant' to allow those called to it to be 'more themselves', to be more completely the people they were intended to be. She concedes that too often the religious life produces quite the opposite effect. However, when religious obedience 'works' it can be 'liberational'.

This point is taken up by Christopher Jamison in a chapter on obedience in his little book *Finding Sanctuary*. He reminds us that 'most people today would probably say that obedience is the diametric opposite of freedom' yet 'the monastic tradition believes that obedience is potentially the greatest expression of human freedom'. He agrees that 'freedom is a core value of modern life' but points out that for many people' their supposedly free choices are driven by hidden agendas'. Fashion is a case in point:

> People are convinced that they are choosing their clothes from endless possibilities... Yet their choices are usually responses to other people's ideas of what they should wear... In contrast, the monastic tradition invites people to listen and then decide freely what voices to follow. It is about who sets the agenda for life. It is ultimately the search to find God's agenda for life. It is the achievement of 'obedient freedom' (Jamison, 2006:72-89).

It is not just in religious communities that people respond to authority with obedience. It will occur wherever people feel that obedience is the 'proper' response. It may occur in respect of the church in the relationship between priest and people. If a priest makes a statement couched in those terms then the people may feel compelled to follow that lead. It may occur in respect of scripture in the relationship between the text and reader. If the words of scripture make demands of the reader then he or she may feel compelled to comply. Such responses may indeed be perfectly credible if human faculties are fully engaged. 'Blind obedience', however, implies a mechanical response. It is hard to give credence to a response in which intellectual, emotional and spiritual faculties play no part.

Allegiance or loyalty to a person

Although 'obedience' has always been thought to be the proper response to God's authority, it can be thoroughly unsatisfactory 'as an ultimate category'. In her book, *The Character of Christian Morality*, Helen Oppenheimer chooses to replace 'obedience' by 'allegiance':

> One can obey with detachment, with reluctance, or even with contempt, and if Christian morality is taken simply as a morality of obedience these unattractive possibilities are apt to be reflected back into it. But when one sincerely gives one's allegiance one is giving one's self, and to believe in God is to believe that there is someone to whom this allegiance can rightly be given in full (Oppenheimer, 1974:55-56).

Oppenheimer sees 'the concept of allegiance, with all its overtones of loyalty rather than of flat conformity' as a way of revealing the true nature of Christian morality. She considers what Christian allegiance might mean in real life.

> For example, the twentieth century has re-opened the question of whether fornication is always wrong. Christian obedience says 'It just is'. Christian compassion says, 'Take each case separately.' Christian allegiance says, equally naively perhaps but more constructively, 'The New Testament gives us a very strong lead against it. There must be some reason for this.' So one is invited to consider what fornication really is, whether there is anything essentially wrong with it which better contraception cannot solve (Oppenheimer, 1974:80).

She goes on to say that 'in view of the biblical insistence on the goodness and importance of the body':

...the point that Christians surely ought to be making is not that there is anything bad about the physical aspects of sex but that it commits one much more deeply than some people would like to think. What is wrong with fornication, therefore, one comes to say, is not what is given but what is held back. The union of two lives which the physical act of sex expresses is here missing (Oppenheimer, 1974:80).

'Allegiance' then ensures that questions remain 'open' and can be thoroughly explored. 'Obedience' insists that questions are 'closed' and that no further debate is permissible. 'Allegiance' is characteristic of an 'open' mind. 'Obedience' is symptomatic of a 'closed' mind.

The distinction between 'allegiance' and 'obedience' can be illustrated in a wider context. To respond in obedience is to see those responses as simply duties to be carried out. If we see regular church attendance as our duty as practising Christians then that is to be applauded but it does not go far enough. To attend services of worship merely from a sense of duty is to seek to absolve ourselves from any fuller commitment. To respond in that way is to do the right thing but from inadequate motives. Those motives are only ever complete when our response arises quite naturally as an expression of our allegiance or loyalty to God.

'Arguments for the sake of heaven'

Even if the proper response to the authority of God is allegiance, it is not always clear what path should be taken. Discussion, debate and argument over fundamental issues have always played a vital role in our journey into truth. In his book, *Authority in the Anglican Communion*, Stephen Sykes claims that 'the phenomenon of internal theological criticism and argument is intrinsic to the life of the Christian Church' (Sykes, 1987:12). In, *Structures for Unity*, John Macquarrie writes that:

I believe that the Anglican Communion exhibits the kind of pluralism which is the mark of a mature adult society and yet that pluralism has not degenerated into sheer chaos but is contained within a framework which is impeccably catholic and has been consciously maintained in continuity with the Church of early centuries (Macquarrie, 1982:114).

In recent years that that pluralism has been severely tested as the 'centre of gravity' of the Anglican Church shifts from its roots in the United Kingdom to the emergent nations of Africa. Powerful voices from these different cultures have a very different 'take' on issues of sexuality and gender, and it is not yet clear that the framework will remain intact. Fragmentation of the Anglican Communion would be a serious blow to the principle of pluralism.

Pluralism is firmly embedded within the Anglican tradition and comprehensiveness has been one of its distinctive features. As has already been mentioned in a previous chapter, the *Final Report* of the Anglican-Roman Catholic International Commission in 1981 outlined agreement on a number of issues including those concerning the notion of a single universal authority (Anglican – Roman Catholic International Commission, 1981).

In a 1983 article in the journal *Theology,* Paul Avis expressed concern about the proposal to 'entrust any single authority with responsibility for articulating the "mind of the Church". He pointed out that, 'Within Anglicanism the human means employed in seeking to arrive at the truth – research, debate, criticism – have been openly acknowledged and indeed encouraged. In the same article, Avis argues that:

...there is a whole new dimension of pluralism that the Commission has failed to take account of, though both Roman Catholics and Anglicans have grappled with the problem, and that is pluralism within the Churches. The reality of pluralism not only between but within the Churches undermines the assumptions of the Report that it is possible for the Church to reach a common mind and feasible for its teaching authority to make decisions that are both relevant and binding (let alone free from error)' (Avis, 1983:406).

In a previous article in the *King's Theological Review*, Avis argues that in the face of attacks on the notion of comprehensiveness within Anglicanism as 'conceptually incoherent and as providing a refuge for woolly thinking, if not intellectual dishonesty', there needs to be a new model which embraces pluralism as:

...learning to distinguish without dividing between, for example, protestant and catholic, individual and corporate, spiritual and formal, transcendent and immanent elements in the wholeness of Christian experience; being guided by the positive affirmations that different traditions have to offer, rather than being diverted by their negative denials; and, finally, looking beneath the surface for the spiritual aspirations and insights that may be veiled by historical or cultural forms (Avis, 1980:62).

His preferred model follows from the historical development of the doctrine of polarity which celebrates 'the quality of living tensions' between different points of view.

Avis also argues persuasively that pluralism is embedded in traditional Anglican faith and practice. 'The doctrine of the transcendence of God implies that no one set of theological statements can adequately describe him, he transcends every attempt to grasp his nature. There thus arises the possibility of a plurality of approaches to the doctrine of God. These may in practice be hard to reconcile or they may appear to be mutually contradictory, but they cannot be ruled out of court simply on grounds of disagreement. Pluralism in the church may be a legitimate response to the mystery of God.' Similarly, 'the bare notion of unity in diversity needs no further initial justification than to point to the presence of this principle in the trinitarian nature of God.' Again, 'biblical scholarship has exposed a plurality of theologies within the Bible itself, both in the Old Testament and in the New', and 'the richness provided by pluriformity helps the church to transcend cultural barriers and protects her from sinking into a culturally insular orthodoxy.' In summary, 'the pluralism of Anglicanism merely mirrors the pluralism of Christianity itself.'(Avis, 1980:55-57).

This is not to deny the essential unity and continuity of the Church's faith but it is to recognise diversity and celebrate difference. As Hans Kung has written in *Structures of the Church*: 'The faith can be the same, the formulations different, indeed contradictory.' He goes on:

Behind such formulations of faith stand different ideas and mental images, concepts, judgements, and conclusions, and different forms of perception, feeling, thinking, volition, speaking, describing, acting, different forms of consciousness of existence and of the objective world, different physio-logical, psychological, aesthetic, linguistic, logical, ethno-logical, historical, ideological, philosophical and religious presuppositions, different individual and collective experi-ences, languages, world views, environmental structures, conception of human nature, and the different traditions of individual peoples, of theological schools, of universities, and of Orders (Kung, 1982:345).

Karl Rahner and Hans Kung have both called for more openness in the Roman Catholic Church. In *Pluralism in Theology and the Unity of the Creed in the Church*, Karl Rahner is pessimistic about 'meaningful communication' in the Roman Catholic Church (Avis, 1983:406). More generally there is clearly frustration within the Church that the call of Second Vatican Council for more conciliarity in the Church continues to go unheeded.

It is also interesting to note that a characteristic form of the relationship with God in Judaism is argument. The Book of Job as a classic example of this genre. Job refuses to accept the conventional wisdom about suffering and insists on taking the argument to God himself. In a recent edition of his weekly newssheet, *Covenant and Conversation*, Jonathan Sacks, the former Chief Rabbi, has written that:

> In Judaism, argument is not an accident but of the essence. The sages gave the phenomenon a name – *argument for the sake of heaven* – and thus a spiritual dignity of its own. They went as far as to portray G-d as saying, about the protagonists and their divergent views, "These and those are the words of the living G-d." G-d lives in the cut and thrust of the House of Study. He does not say: "X is right, and Y is wrong." He does not deliver the verdict: He empowers His sages to do that. The word of the Lord gives rise to the wars of the Lord – but wars without violence, bloodshed or conquest' (Sacks, 2006).

In his book, *The Authority of Divine Love*, Richard Harries comments that 'sometimes in Jewish humour, a humour which has helped Jews to live through their tragic history with courage and dignity, this argument with God takes daring forms':

> ...in stores about Auschwitz, for example, in which a Rabbi and God dispute about who has gone too far, man in perpetrating such evil or God in allowing it to fall upon his people. Into our relationship to God we bring all that we honestly are and feel; and our ultimate response to him is achieved by way of struggle. It is very different from parade-ground concepts

of obedience (Harries, 1983:12).

'The authority of divine love'

In the same book, Richard Harries writes, 'The idea of authority is taken seriously by Christians not just because God exists and because he has revealed himself to us, but also because we see in that revelation the mind and heart of love'.

> Authority implies and entails obedience. At the heart of Christian discipleship, for both individual Christians and the Church as a whole, is obedience to Christ. But the phrase 'obedience to Christ' can give an oversimplified and therefore false view of what is involved. It brings to mind the picture of someone giving orders and everyone else obeying them without question. Our relationship with God is not like that. There is much wrestling to discover whether what purports to be the will of God really is so (Harries, 1983:12).

This distinction between common usage of the word 'authority' and its use in this context needs to be spelt out:

> Arbitrary fiats and peremptory commands, however confi-dently uttered by however a powerful body, whether human or divine, have no authority whatever. The sole ultimate authority is that of divine love: the heart and mind of God revealed in Christ. The only obedience that has moral justifi-cation springs from a recognition of this love, which elicits a freely given allegiance. On these terms, the acceptance of authority and obedience has an essential place in the life of the Church (Harries, 1983:15).

We are so conditioned by common usage of the word 'authority' that we need to be quite clear what the 'authority of divine love' actually means:

The Christian wants to assert that the only true basis for authority is a divine love that calls forth our wholehearted moral assent. We are moral beings, and in the end the only reason for giving our allegiance to something is not that it is more powerful, more confident or more guilt-inducing, but simply that it is the fount and focus of all that we value (Harries, 1983:9).

So much for authority but what of power? As we have already noted, authority without power is impotent.

It might be said that in creating the world God took a great risk, for the only power he uses is that of suffering love. He makes himself vulnerable to the universe to the extent of being captive to it. The cross is the only instrument he uses for bringing us to our right minds, and the resurrection is to be seen primarily in terms of a new understanding of God brought about by the cross (Harries, 1983:10) .

In a journal article, *The Authority of Love*, Bishop Butler draws a distinction between the 'authority of constraint' and the 'authority of appeal'. The former operates by the threat of punishment; the latter operates by free response. He writes:

And there is one thing that we know with certainty about love: it cannot succeed by constraint; it can only reach its aim by appeal, by courtship, by "wooing"... To have caught a glimpse of absolute and infinite love is to be haunted for ever afterwards by its appeal, until the surrender is made and freely and deliberately, we begin to learn the lesson of recip-rocal love (Butler, 1990).

In his essay, *The Authority of Love*, Edward Scott examines the implications for the church. The church certainly claims authority, but on what grounds?

Supreme authority should be love as this was the supreme
authority for Jesus. It seems to follow that the church will only
be able to act with authority as it becomes an accepting, loving
supportive challenging community, a community held
together by the "bonds of affection". Such a community
requires some structure, order and form which are not ends in
themselves but the means that enable the Church to be and to
do what it is called to be and to do (Scott, 1987).

'Service is the key to authority'

Jack Dominian, the highly respected psychiatrist, claims that, 'in
the realm of authority the Christian community as a whole has
failed to read the signs of the times accurately and its leaders...
have made serious errors'. He goes on, 'The reasons for this
failure are threefold'. I make no apology for repeating them:

The first has been to associate the Kingdom of God with an
authoritarian system, dependent on the use of authority as a
source of power, generating feelings of fear and guilt in its
adherents which are foreign to the message of the Christian
Gospel, where authority is seen primarily as service and
where the essential message of love is incompatible with fear,
a point beautifully and succinctly made by John in 1 John 4:
16-18.
    The second is the failure to discriminate between
supporting law and order in the community... and the
evolution of human relationships from positions which
belong to early childhood where inequality, fear and dependency predominate, to the more mature later stages in which
maturity is seeking equality of personal worth in the presence
of differentiating capacities and characteristics.
    The third, and in some ways the most serious, failure of all

is that the Christian community has fostered ideals which have encouraged the characteristics of early childhood emotional immaturity, and have perpetuated that immaturity in its various structures, particularly the priesthood (Dominian, 1976:81).

In an article entitled, *Authority and Paternalism,* in the journal, *The Way,* Dominian looks at 'the structure of the family for a clarification and understanding of the origin of authority in the human personality' and its manifestation in the institutional church, most notably the Roman Catholic Church of which Dominian is a member. He reminds us of the parallels between the father-figure in the family and in the church, whether it be the local parish priest or the Pope himself. He reminds us of Freud's claim that the projection of the earthly father into the heavenly one creates the 'significant other' that we think we need for survival.

He identifies two conflicting understandings of the role of authority in the growth and development of children.

One principle difference between authority used as a means of growth through the establishment of rules and regulations which lie external to the child, and authority as a service, offering to the child the means of acquiring a separate, independent, inner-directed existence which relies on itself for direction, control and judgment of behaviour. The trust provided by the parents has to become the trust the child learns to place in itself, thus avoiding a life-long dependence on 'significant others' for survival (Dominian, 1972).

He concludes his article by stating that 'everyone would agree that service is the hallmark of the use of authority in the New Testament. But service for what?'

Surely, the authoritarian philosophy would reply, to maintain a relationship between man and God which acknowledges the latter's transcendence, omnipotence, absolutism, and man's dependence, helplessness, sinfulness: and therefore the superior-inferior, master-pupil, parent-child relationship (Dominian, 1972).

On the contrary, Dominian argues:

The more each person realizes his potential, the more he achieves autonomy, self-acceptance, inner-directed purpose and meaning, and a love of self which is not a reflection of selfishness or egotism but a plenitude which is available to others in and through love. Such a concept of growth, personal or spiritual, owes nothing to the need to hold on to a 'significant other' for survival, as Freud postulated, but an identification with a significant other called God, who invites us to realize our potential and become like him, not in absolute power and authority, but in absolute love, which is his nature (Dominian, 1972).

We are reminded of the familiar words from the gospel according to Mark:

You know that among the Gentiles those whom they recognize as their rulers lord it over them, and their great ones are tyrants over them. But it is not so among you; but whoever wishes to become great among you must be your servant, and whoever wishes to be first among you must be slave of all. For the Son of Man came not to be served but to serve, and to give his life a ransom for many (Mark 10:42-45).

In his book, *Authority: A Christian interpretation of the psychological evolution of authority,* Jack Dominian writes that 'service is the key to authority'.

But service means personal availability, and the authority of Christ, as indeed of every Christian, is to be identified in the rendering of service which makes the self available to others (Dominian, 1976:92).

This personal availability 'is dependent on wholeness'.

We cannot give to others what we do not possess ourselves. Thus availability depends on the greatest possible development of our wholeness. Man is a unity of his physical, psychological, social and spiritual realities. Our wholeness depends on the greatest possible harmonious realisation of the conscious and unconscious potential of these realities (Dominian, 1976:92)

The realisation of this potential depends on our self-esteem, 'on the affirmative acceptance of ourselves'.

There is no point in having the most powerful body or mind, the greatest social aptitude if we *feel* insignificant, helpless, bad, inadequate or unworthy. If we do not feel good, we nullify whatever objective goodness and talent we own (Dominian, 1976:92).

It also depends on empathy, on the awareness of 'the inner world of another person'.

The greater our awareness of the inner world of another person, the greater will be our ability to respond accurately to their mood, physical and emotional needs, to grasp their unexpressed yearnings, to clarify their confusion and facilitate the emergence of themselves without the intrusion of our own interpretation of reality (Dominian, 1976:93).

Finally, service can only be truly effective if there is equality and friendship in relationships. It is characteristic of many examples of authority that one party has power over the other, and there is an intrinsic inequality between the two. In the authority of service, there is no such inequality. In his life, death and resurrection, Jesus became equal with us.

> This is my commandment, that you love one another as I have loved you. No one has greater love than this, to lay down one's life for one's friends. You are my friends if you do what I command you" (John 15:12-14).

Why do we respond as we do?

Introduction

In the previous chapter we explored some of the ways in which we respond to authority. In this chapter we look at why we respond to that authority as we do. This means that we shall be looking at motives and at the insights of psychology.

Psychological foundations for our response

Although some psychologists and religious people are sceptical or downright hostile to any notion of a psychology *of* religion, others have embraced the possibility that, despite the difficulties, the insights of psychology can be applied in this way. In his book, *Psychology and Religion*, Andrew Fuller outlines the point of view adopted by a number of psychologists who have taken this approach seriously and who have contributed significantly to our understanding of what Gordon Allport calls the 'religious sentiment'. Fuller describes these different approaches as like the different paths that can be taken across a landscape. Each path discovers only part of the landscape and only a multitude of paths will ever cover all the ground (Fuller, 1994).

In their book, *The Psychology of Religion: An Empirical Approach*, Hood, Silka et al describe the approaches to the particular question of the psychological foundations of religious sentiment as falling into two distinct groups – the 'defensive-protective tradition' and the 'growth-realisation tradition'. The first approach has a negative emphasis and relates to problems associated with human shortcomings, weakness and inadequacy. It is an approach that has generated considerable research. The second approach is more positive and relates to growth, development and progress. But it has been more difficult to operationalise in research because the concepts are less easy to define. The first approach is that generally taken by those with an empirical or behavioural outlook. The second approach is taken by those with a humanistic or phenomenological point of view (Hood, Spilka et al. 1996).

The 'defensive-protective tradition'

In this tradition, religion satisfies a psychological need. When people are unable to make sense of the world or to control events around them, they become fearful and seek reassurance. Fear arises from human shortcomings, weakness or inadequacy. Reassurance comes with religious faith and praxis. Although psychologists disagree about the detail of the mechanisms at work here, many attribute adult behaviour to be continuation of their behaviour as a child. Foremost amongst those who take this view is Sigmund Freud (1856-1939).

Freud and the numinous as an 'illusion'

Freud was a serious student of religion despite his antagonism towards its traditional manifestations. For him, all religious ideas are illusions; they are products of the imagination which bring enormous relief from the stress of daily life. In the face of stress, adults are weak and helpless as they were as children. In childhood they turn to their father for protection and care. In adulthood they turn to the father-figure, to God. The childhood and adulthood situations are, therefore, fundamentally related; our helpless situation as adults is simply a continuation of our helplessness as a child. Adult religion is therefore infantile and shows infantile characteristics. We become dependent on the father-figure and religion becomes a 'prop'.

Freud finds children and adults to be ambivalent towards the father. On the one hand, they feel the need for the father's care and protection through love. On the other, they fear him and are wary of how he may respond to them. This ambivalence is characteristic of the immaturity of childhood in respect of a real father. It is also characteristic of the weakness of the adult as he or she constructs a father-figure to fulfil the same function. In one sense, dependence and fear are both needs. The father is both the provider of care and protection, and also the provider of justice and punishment. These characteristics come together in the notion of authority.

Freud is optimistic that infantilism in religion can be overcome. As Fuller explains, Freud believes that people will eventually be able to see things as they are rather than as how they imagine them to be. This will come with the 'primacy of the intellect' as only science can provide knowledge of reality. As 'the intellect conquers the imagination', so religious beliefs will wither away. 'Freud allows no court of appeals above reason' (Fuller, 1994:39-46).

As we shall see later, Freud's apparent fixation with the role of the father is not shared by many other psychologists. Some would wish to emphasise the dual role of both father and mother in the development of religious sentiment. Others would point to a whole host of other factors.

Whatever the influences, however, it is clear that even if infantilism in religious matters among adults is not inevitable, as Freud suggests, it is an ever present danger. In his book, *Authority*, Jack Dominian draws attention to our predisposition to return to infantile responses under stress.

> For obvious reasons, namely that all response to authority begins in its most elementary, blind and automatic form, we tend to return to that form under stress or uncertainty. It is the most deeply ingrained response and both society and religion have tended to rely heavily on this mode and to turn to this early level when they have been under attack or threat (Dominian, 1976:42).

Whatever the source, there are many psychological factors which clearly have a significant bearing on 'religious sentiment'. In *The*

Nature and Limits of Authority, Richard De George has noted that:

> ...people do not always grant authority, and they probably
> rarely submit to it only for rational reasons. The psychological
> reasons for accepting authority are equally important and
> yield correlative psychological sources of authority (De
> George, 1985:95).

He goes on to identify four qualities that can be 'both a reason for
accepting authority and a source of authority' – fear, need, habit
and the herd instinct.

Fear and anxiety

It is not easy to define what is understood by 'fear' in this context,
but it may be possible to resolve the difficulty by placing it in the
context of our total response to God himself. It was Rudolf Otto
who, in *The Idea of the Holy*, spoke of the special way in which we
respond to the numinous. He writes:

> Let us consider the deepest and most fundamental element in
> all strong and sincerely felt religious emotion. Faith unto
> salvation, trust, love – all these are there. But over and above
> these is an element which may also on occasion, quite apart
> from them, profoundly affect us and occupy the mind with a
> well-nigh bewildering strength... Let us follow it up with
> every effort of sympathy and imaginative intuition wherever
> it is to be found... If we do so we shall find we are dealing
> with something for which there is only one appropriate
> expression, *mysterium tremendum*'.
>
> 'Tremor' is in itself merely the perfectly familiar and
> natural emotion of 'fear'. But here the term is taken, aptly
> enough but still only by analogy, to denote a quite specific
> kind of emotional response, wholly distinct from that of being
> afraid, though it so far resembles it that the analogy of fear

may be used to throw light on its nature' The closest word seems to be 'awe' which is 'the feeling which, emerging in the mind of primeval man, forms the starting-point for the entire religious development in history' (Otto, 1958:12-24).

Building on this understanding, Otto summaries the elements of *mysterium tremendum* as 'awe', 'power' and 'urgency'. Otto did not pursue his interest in the role of fear in the religious life. It was only when the role of the unconscious was recognised that momentum was restored.

Freud's interest in religion led to extensive research in its psychoanalytical interpretation, but this work gained the reputation of being hostile to religion because it reduced it to infantile or neurotic tendencies like anxiety, depression or obsession. Oskar Pfister (1873-1956) a Swiss pastor and psycho-analyst, and a lifelong friend of Freud, suggested that the insights of psychoanalysis could serve religious faith and practice more positively. In *Christianity and Fear* (Pfister, 1948), Pfister maintains that:

...neurotic trends in religion, whether on the individual or the group level, lead to an overemphasis on dogma and the replacement of love by hate. Only by returning love to the supreme position will Christianity regain the spirit of Jesus. We may employ the techniques and insights of psycho-analysis... without subscribing to its underlying philosophy or Freud's own views of religion' (Wulff, 1997:33).

Pfister's guiding principle is enshrined in the text, 'There is no fear in love, but perfect love casts out fear' (1John 4:18). For Pfister fear is caused by the 'disturbances of love' (Pfister, 1948:46).

For Pfister, the psychoanalytic theory of neurosis could help explain why fear has played such a prominent part in the history of the Christian tradition. Following a survey of Judaism and its preoccupation with the Law, he turns to the work of Jesus.

> Jesus wanted to liberate the Jews and mankind in general from the domination of fear caused by guilt... of the spirit of compulsion emanating from the Rabbis and the Pharisees, and of the rule of sin; he wished to give them a new love – a radiant love illuminating life, free from fear and giving them strength to fulfil the divine will to love... Jesus displaced conscience, a strict authority promoting the formation of fear and of compulsion, in favour of love, a milder and kindly authority' (Pfister, 1948:209-216).

The transformation achieved by Jesus was only possible because he was 'transparent to the deity' in way that was not possible for those who followed. Paul, for example, appears to have had a complex personality with a neurotic disposition and to have been unwilling or unable to eliminate fear from his preaching. His words are obscure and at times contradictory. On the one hand, he writes to the Philippians:

> Therefore, my beloved, just as you have always obeyed me, not only in my presence, but much more now in my absence, work out your own salvation with fear and trembling (Philip 2:12).

On the other hand, his message to the Romans conveys a very different impression:

> For you did not receive a spirit of slavery to fall back into fear, but you have received a spirit of adoption (Romans 8:15).

It is possible that Paul saw both positive and negative aspects of obedience and fear in the gospel he felt compelled to preach, and that different groups and circumstances demanded different 'takes' on that gospel. It is also possible that tensions existed between intellectual assent and emotional disposition within his own personality, tensions which too often overflowed into his teaching.

Tensions and weaknesses within individuals and groups were responsible for a huge increase in demands for obedience and in fear of consequences amongst believers as the persecuted followers of the early decades gave way to the institutional church of subsequent centuries. As the power and influence of the Papacy increased so did demands for obedience and sanctions against dissenters. In due course:

...the Church set up rigid moral and religious rules and prohibitions; it impressed on the mind horrible images from early childhood onwards, and it canalized the vital impulses in a compulsion-neurotic direction, damaging in the process that love which Christ had designated as the sole criterion. In this way it created conditions which inevitably induced a new and heavier fear and consequently in their turn inevitably called into being an unceasing struggle against fear operating through symbols and ritual (Pfister, 1948:313-314).

Fear was both caused and resolved within the vast edifice that was the Roman Catholic Church. Causes of fear included demonic images, the prospect of hell and moral prohibitions. Fear could be resolved by attendance at mass, in confession and in the promise of heaven. Fear and obedience amongst the masses were key weapons in the service of power and control exercised by the hierarchy. The authoritarianism and corruption within the Church was a major cause of the Reformation.

The 'culture' of fear that existed within the Roman Catholic Church before the Reformation was different in kind from that which emerged afterwards within Protestantism. This had much to do with the fact that whereas Roman Catholicism was largely homogeneous and had a single focus in the Papacy, Protestantism was more heterogeneous and followed the teaching of individual reformers, most notably Luther, Zwingli and Calvin. The nature of the very different fear that was generated in future generations of the Protestant Churches was the result not only of the teaching of these men and their followers, but the result of their individual temperaments and the way they tackled their task. They were very different men and spawned very different traditions. Zwingli was more disposed towards love and managed his fear more successfully than either Luther or Calvin so it on them that we must focus our attention in this book.

Luther's upbringing was severe. He suffered from abuse both at home and at school and grew to fear his parents, his teachers and his God. He was terrified of the wrath of God and frantically sought ways to earn His grace and favour. Although he realised that grace came from God, he was determined to earn this grace. He was obsessed by the need to confess and was tormented by the thought that his confession had not been complete. A breakthrough came when he realised that man gains the grace of God not by his deeds but by his faith, and that this faith is not a meritorious action on the part of man but a gift from God. For Luther this was a great relief, but it did not remove the burden of fear altogether. Alongside the gift of grace was the threat of justice and fear remained. Perhaps because of his predisposition to fear, Luther was never able to fully embrace the love of Jesus.

Fear was the foundation of Calvin's personal religion as it had been for Luther. His focus on the sovereignty of God and his promotion of the doctrine of predestination ensured that love was almost extinguished in his scheme of things. The implication of his teaching seemed to be that there are a small number of elect whom God loves, but that there are a larger number of reprobates whom God hates. Calvin's severe and uncompromising attitude led to a reign of terror in Geneva as he sought to subjugate everything and everybody to his particularly view of how religious and secular life should function. He achieved much, but in a climate of fear.

It is clear that the reformers achieved much in their recasting of the faith. But in doing so they could be said to have merely replaced one kind of fear by another and so failed to clear the way for love to take its course. Subsequent events show that the climate was ripe for new fears to emerge and new ways of dealing with them.

Need and dependence

In, *The Nature and Limits of Authority*, de George expands on 'need' as one of the psychological reasons for accepting authority. He writes, 'Need is a source of authority; it can provide both justification of authority and a motive for accepting it'.

> People rely on epistemic authorities because they do not have the time, energy, opportunity, or competence to develop or discover for themselves the knowledge that they need and want. People rely on the competence of others for the goods and services that they need but cannot produce for themselves. Because of the need to act in concert with others in order to achieve certain ends, they submit to the coordinating direction or orders of an authority. The weak feel the need to rely on and to submit their wills to authority for protection against the strong. Need serves both as a source for the development of structures of authority and as a psychological reason for accepting authority (De George, 1985:96).

It is important to examine these needs more systematically. In his book, *Psychology of Religion: Classic and Contemporary*, David Wulf outlines Abraham Maslow's description of a 'hierarchy of needs':

At the bottom of the hierarchy are the *physiological needs*, such as for food, water, and sleep… When the physiological needs are more or less satisfactorily met, a new set emerges and becomes dominant: the *safety needs*, for protection, security, predictability, structure, order, and so on… At the third level of the hierarchy we find *belongingness and love needs*, including the needs for roots, for home and family, for neighbourhood and friends, for contact and intimacy. *Esteem needs* emerge next and encompass the desire for adequacy, competence, achievement, independence, and freedom as well as for deserved recognition, appreciation, and respect from others (Maslow, 1970) (Wulf, 1997:606).

These represent the 'lower' or 'deficiency' needs 'because they are actuated by the absence of the needed object'.

The 'higher' or 'growth' needs form the fifth level of the hierarchy, the generic need for *self-actualisation*. Ordinarily appearing after only after the prior satisfaction of the other four needs, the peculiarly human desire to actualize potentialities, to attain fuller knowledge of one's nature and higher levels of integration, is the least prepotent of the needs and the least debilitating if unmet. In contrast to deficiency needs, which subside when they are satisfied, growth needs are intensified by gratification (Maslow, 1970) (Wulf, 1997:606).

It is important to understand what Maslow means by 'self-actualization'. Although there are clearly individual differences, it would appear that those 'rare, healthy and inevitably older individuals whose lives are animated by self-actualization generally resemble one another in significant ways':

Briefly summarised, the most important characteristics of self-actualising persons are said to be the following: more accurate perception and acceptance of reality, including human nature; spontaneity, freshness of appreciation, and creativeness in everyday activities; relative detachment from the immediate physical and social environment and from the culture at large; deeper, more satisfying interpersonal relations, most likely with a small number of other self-actualizing persons; strong feelings of identification and sympathy for all other human beings; democratic (non-authoritarian) character structure; non-hostile, philosophical humour; centeredness in problems lying outside themselves and reflecting a broad framework of values; clear moral and ethical standards that are consistently applied; and the felt resolution of apparent dichotomies or pairs of opposites (Maslow, 1970) (Wulf, 1997:607).

Maslow goes to identify one other characteristic of self-actualization. He 'found that it was fairly common for his subjects to report mystical experiences' and 'to dissociate such ecstatic states from all traditional religious interpretations and, on the contrary, to emphasize their entirely natural origin, Maslow called them peak experiences':

Associated with a variety of contexts, peak experiences are marked by feelings of wholeness and integration, of relatively egoless fusion with the world, of spontaneity and effortlessness, of fully existing in the here and now. Individuals not only feel more self-activated, more fully functioning, more creative, but objective observers are likely to perceive them that way as well. Profoundly satisfying in themselves, peak experiences may revolutionize the lives in which they occur. They contribute to the feeling that life is truly worth living (Maslow, 1964, 1968) (Wulf, 1997:608).

However, not everyone achieves self-actualization or peak

experiences and many have needs which mitigate against any possibility of achieving the growth to which they may aspire. In his collection of essays entitled, *Cycles of Affirmation*, Jack Dominian describes the part played by the authority structures of the Roman Catholic Church:

> In the last decade or so the changes in the Church have made us aware how much the authoritarian structure of the past acted as a refuge for personalities who moved from one dependent relationship, in which their lives were organised by parents, to another similar relationship in which the Church took over the role of the parental figure instructing them and freeing them from the responsibility of initiative. Similarly, a high percentage of priests and nuns leaving the Church at the present time are men and women who found their way to these vocations not because they had a genuine calling but because the structure of the priesthood and of the religious life could contain this emotional dependence which, although totally unconscious, was their primary need. Because of a marked change in the atmosphere within the Church, coinciding for many with their own maturation out of such needs, such people find their old way of life totally irrelevant to their newly discovered identity (Dominian, 1975:5).

There are, of course, many within the Church who are unable to reach this kind of maturity because of the way in which the Church 'infantilises' its people. In a letter to me, following an inquiry about his current writings, Jack Dominian wrote:

> My interest in subsequent writing has been to focus on the relationship between the authoritarian approach of the Catholic Church and the consequent infantilisation of its people. My main theme of an enduring dependence in adulthood of people who are in authoritarian systems of

course continues in all my writings with all the damaging implications (Dominian, 2006).

What is true of the Catholic Church is also true of other churches where the authoritarian structures are perhaps less obvious but where dependence flourishes nonetheless.

Habit

De George also writes of 'habit' as one of the psychological reasons for accepting authority:

Habit also motivates the acceptance of authority. We are taught to live with the authority structures of the societies into which we are born. By habit we unquestioningly accept them, unless something upsets the established order or circumstances force us to re-examine what we accept. Inertia inclines us not to change things unless they become intolerable. We have neither the time nor the energy to question everything. The acceptance of established authority frees us to be creative in other areas. Habit does not justify accepting authority, for we can ask why the habit was established in the first place; but habit is a reason why many people automatically and without question do accept many kinds of authority (De George, 1985:96).

In 1887, William James, one of the 'fathers' of modern psychology, wrote *Habit*, an essay, later published as a book, on how our behavioral patterns shape who we are and what we often refer to as character and personality. He writes, 'When we look at living creatures from an outward point of view, one of the first things that strike us is that they are bundles of habits':

Any sequence of mental action which has been frequently repeated tends to perpetuate itself; so that we find ourselves automatically prompted to think, feel, or do what we have been before accustomed to think, feel, or do, under like circumstances, without any consciously formed purpose, or anticipation of results (James, 1914).

James appears to take a somewhat jaundiced view as he describes habit as 'the enormous fly-wheel of society, its most precious conservative agent'. He goes on:

It alone is what keeps us all within the bounds of ordinance, and saves the children of fortune from the envious uprisings of the poor. It alone prevents the hardest and most repulsive walks of life from being deserted by those brought up to tread therein... It dooms us all to fight out the battle of life upon the lines of our nurture or our early choice, and to make the best of a pursuit that disagrees, because there is no other for which we are fitted, and it is too late to begin again. It keeps different social strata from mixing... You see the little lines of cleavage running through the character, the tricks of thought, the preju-dices, the ways of the 'shop,' in a word, from which the man can by-and-by no more escape than his coat-sleeve can suddenly fall into a new set of folds. On the whole, it is best he should not escape. It is well for the world that in most of us, by the age of thirty, the character has set like plaster, and will never soften again (James, 1914).

He goes on to say that the key to the acquisition of good habits is education, and that, once acquired, good habits free us to use our brains for the more demanding decision making activities in our lives:

...we must make automatic and habitual, as early as possible, as many useful actions as we can, and guard against the growing into ways that are likely to be disadvantageous to us, as we should guard against the plague. The more of the details of our daily life we can hand over to the effortless custody of automatism, the more our higher powers of mind will be set free for their own proper work. There is no more miserable human being than one in whom nothing is habitual but indecision, and for whom the lighting of every cigar, the drinking of every cup, the time of rising and going to bed every day, and the beginning of every bit of work, are subjects of express volitional deliberation (James, 1914).

The difficulty is that the absence of decision making that characterises habitual behaviour can sometimes extend to those areas where critical faculties ought to be engaged. This applies particularly to religion:

Though James thought of religion as much more than the product of simple learning, in a critical sense he might have had in mind the way most people seem to acquire and express their faith mechanically. Parents teach it to their children and these lessons are reinforced by society through the fact that births, marriages, death, and virtually every noteworthy personal and social event is solemnized by religious institutions, rituals, language, and concepts (Hood, Spilka, Hunsberger, & Gorsuch, 1996:23).

This is particularly true in the USA where the patterns of religious faith and practice are deeply imbedded in the culture.

U.S. society possess a generalized religious atmosphere, a 'civil religion' that is integral to public social and political life. The U.S. milieu tells its inhabitants from early childhood that it is simply 'un-American' not to believe in God... Americans are supposed to believe without question and know enough not to think too deeply about these issues. This is a habitual religion, a mechanical religion, a convenient religion. It is a faith to which all are expected to give reverent assent, but one that will not otherwise interfere with people's lives. It is a religion of unthinking, automatic habits (Hood, Hunsberger, & Gorsuch, 1996:23).

The pattern of religious practice in the UK is very different and habit may not be so well ingrained but within the worshipping life of the church the response can sometimes be mindless.

A priest checks the microphone before the start of a church service with the words, 'can you hear me?' to which he receives the response, 'and also with you'!

The Herd Instinct

De George writes as follows of the 'herd instinct' as the fourth in his list of the psychological reasons for accepting authority:

The herd instinct is another reason why many people accept authority. If a group accepts X as an authority or if it submits to X, there is a strong tendency for each member of the group to do likewise. The acceptance of X by each person is reinforced by the acceptance by the others... The herd instinct, by itself, provides no valid ground for accepting authority; but it provides an impetus for accepting as adequate those grounds that are accepted by others (De George, 1985:96).

The notion of the 'herd mentality' arises most prominently in the writings of the German philosopher Friedrich Nietzsche. Nietzsche is notoriously difficult to cope with as a serious commentator of the Christian enterprise but he is nonetheless an important voice not least because he challenges us to confront some uncomfortable truths about Christian faith and praxis.

In the Introduction to her book, *The SPCK Introduction to Nietzsche*, Lucy Huskinson writes about her approach:

This book does not pretend that Nietzsche's thought can be aligned with Christianity, and neither does it adopt clever tricks of interpretation to portray Nietzsche as a closet Christian. Indeed, the sole fact that Nietzsche explicitly rejects Christ makes any such attempt futile and fundamentally flawed. What this book does attempt to do, however, is to outline Nietzsche's search for, and explanation of, authentic divinity, through his destruction of what he deems to be the dehumanising and corrupt values of Christianity, and his subsequent creation of a 'new' faith grounded in the affirmation of life (Huskinson, 2009:xiii).

The 'affirmation of life' underpins Nietzsche's philosophy and anything which gets in the way of what it means to 'live' is condemned. He takes issue with the idea that there are 'objective truths, which tell us how things really are, and imperatives, which tell us how we ought to behave'.

He attacks Christianity for what he believes are its crimes against life. In particular, for setting up in contradistinction to life, with its promise – through death – of a better world beyond human life... He regards Christianity as a delusory system of thought that manipulates human life according to its power-hungry ends (Huskinson, 2009:2).

He wants us to engage in the fullness of life without the constraints which encourage submission and the repression of creativity.

Those who would rather seek comfort, peace and safety in the community of truths and values (an approach Nietzsche calls 'herd-thinking') than in the tension and strife of individual creation may find themselves happy, but they can never be satisfied (Huskinson, 2009:6).

Nietzsche, therefore, regards orthodox Christianity as a 'herd' mentality and orthodox Christians as 'slaves' to its precepts. Even if we reject his radical approach, there is food for thought in his philosophy.

A very different approach is adopted in a famous book, *Instincts of the Herd in Peace and War,* written in the early years of the twentieth century by W Trotter. He wrote that 'the herd instinct is the root cause of man's religious behaviour'. He goes on:

> Religion has always been to man an intensely serious matter, and when we realize its biological significance we can see that this is due to a deeply ingrained need of his mind. The individual of a gregarious species can never be truly independent and self-sufficient. Natural selection has ensured that as an individual he must have an abiding sense of incompleteness, which, as thought develops in complexity, will come to be more and more abstractly expressed. This is the psychological germ which expresses itself in the religious feelings, in the desire for completion, for mystical union, for incorporation with the infinite, which are all provided for in Christianity (Trotter, 1921:50).

In, *Escape From Freedom,* Eric Fromm offers 'an analysis of the phenomenon of man's anxiety engendered by the breakdown of the Medieval World in which, in spite of many dangers, he felt himself secure and safe'. In the Foreword, he writes,

> It is the thesis of this book that modern man, freed from the bonds of pre-individualistic society, which simultaneously gave him security and limited him, has not gained freedom in the positive sense of the realization of his individual self; that is, the expression of his intellectual, emotional and sensuous potentialities. Freedom, though it has brought him indepen-

dence and rationality, has made him isolated and, thereby, anxious and powerless. This isolation is unbearable and the alternatives he is confronted with are either to escape from the burden of his freedom into new dependencies and submission, or to advance to the full realization of positive freedom which is based upon the uniqueness and individuality of man (Fromm, 1994:x).

So, inevitably many follow the 'herd'. The 'herd' is willing to accept the loss of freedom of autonomy as the price to pay for accepting the slave belief in the necessity of submitting to powerful leaders. Fromm illustrates this by reference to the rise of Fascism but that is but one extreme example of a much more general trend.

Fromm claims that 'we are fascinated by the growth of freedom from powers *outside* ourselves and are blinded to the fact of *inner* restraints, compulsions and fears, which tend to undermine the meaning of the victories freedom has won against its traditional enemies'.

We are proud that in his conduct of life man has become free from external authorities, which tell him what to do and what not to do. We neglect the role of the anonymous authorities like public opinion and 'common sense', which are so powerful because of our profound readiness to conform to the expectations everybody has about ourselves and our equally profound fear of being different (Fromm, 1994:105).

The 'profound fear of being different' is all too easy to observe amongst members the Christian Church. Too many people are afraid of speaking out against a theology that desperately needs to be recast for the modern world, an ecclesiology that that needs to become grounded in the realities of people's lives and aspirations, and an outreach that should be more concerned with human dignity and social justice in this world than with individual salvation and ultimate destiny in the next.

Fromm identifies 'automaton conformity' as one of the ways in which we cope with freedom. 'The discrepancy between 'I' and the world disappears and with the conscious fear of aloneness and powerlessness':

> An individual ceases to be himself; he adopts entirely the kind of personality offered to him by cultural patterns; and he therefore becomes exactly as all others are and as they expect him to be (Fromm, 1994:184)

The 'growth-realisation tradition'

Despite the strength of the 'defensive-protective' tradition within the psychology profession, a number of professionals have proposed an alternative and more positive approach – the 'growth-realisation tradition'. In their survey of this approach in *The Psychology of Religion*, Hood, Spilka et al. have written:

> Increasingly, the humanistic and phenomenological psychologies support the idea that people have the potential to create, grow, develop, progress, and become ever more competent and able... Religion now becomes self-enhancement, growth, realisation, actualisation, the broad-ening of experiential horizons This accords well with Tillich's perception that "faith as ultimate concern is an act of the total personality"' (Hood, Spilka et al. 1996:22).

This more positive attitude towards the psychological processes involved in religious faith first arose in the work of Carl Gustav Jung (1875-1961).

Jung and the numinous as a 'psychological fact'

Despite Jung's close association with Freud over a number of years, and despite their common interest in psychodynamic processes, they parted company on the causes of these processes. For Freud, all psychological process, including the religious sentiment, were based on instinct. For Jung, there was an independent spiritual source arising from 'archetypes' in the unconscious. In Fuller's introduction to the work of Jung, he explains that, for Jung, 'the mind is possessed of specific principles of its own' called archetypes. These archetypes together with instincts constitute the 'collective unconscious' which 'represents in condensed form untold years of human experience, constituting in each of us the sum total of the psychological functioning of our ancestors'. These inherited archetypes 'express themselves in consciousness in the form of universal symbols or myths... structure all its experiences, and initiate its far-reaching transformations'. He goes on, 'Charged with archetypal power, symbols introduce the zest of the divine into consciousness, turning every human life into a spiritual adventure of meaning'... 'Spirit, then, has a life of its own and is every bit as universal as instinct'. Jung therefore feels able to explore the life of the spirit 'on its own terms' (Fuller, 1994:71).

For Jung, this 'zest of the divine' arises because archetypes possess the quality of the 'numinous'. 'Numinous' is a term first used by Rudolf Otto in his book, *The Idea of the Holy* (Otto, 1958) It is a difficult word to define but it is intended to convey the sense of the holy, that which invokes feelings of awe. The numinous is an experience of the divine, of 'gods'. It is internal to the psyche and Jung has nothing to say about what may or may not exist externally. The psyche contains a kind of 'pantheon' of gods; Jung sometimes uses God as a synonym for the collective unconscious. His understanding of religion is therefore not orthodox. He has nothing to say about the transcendent God of the Christian tradition.

For Jung, the 'adventure of meaning' is a process of, what he calls, 'individuation'. It is the way an individual becomes what

he is destined to be. It is a process of extricating oneself from the
domination of both internal and external influences. It reaches its
climax in the experience of what Jung calls the 'self'. The 'self' is
personality in all its wholeness and it is our task in life to work
towards that goal. It brings with it a sense not only of wholeness
but of timelessness, of immortality, of God. God, for Jung, is a
'psychological fact' representing that which is of supreme power
and value in an individual's life and looms large in their psyche.
In a famous television interview with John Freeman, Jung was
asked if he *believed* in God and he replied: "I *know*".

Growth

This more positive and optimistic view of human personality is
explored further by humanitarian psychologists who have inves-
tigated the potential in people to grow, develop and progress.
Abraham Maslow (1908-1970) describes the 'wonderful possibilities and inscrutable depths' of human nature.

Maslow rejects the orthodox view that our primary
motivation consists only in satisfying basic instinctive needs and
drives. He also rejects the notion that only those things that are
manifested universally throughout the species can be regarded as
innate. This view claims, for example, that the hunger for food is
innate because it appears everywhere, but the desire for justice is
not because it is not universally expressed.

Malsow's alternative view is described by Richard Lowry in
his Foreword to the book, *Towards a Psychology of Being*. He claims
that we have a host of inborn motives all jostling for position and
that these motives are hierarchical according to urgency and
intensity. So the 'higher' human motives are just as innate and the
fact that they are not universal does not mean that they are deriv-
ative. They are rooted in the core of our personality but for much
of the time become eclipsed by more biologically urgent motives.
These 'deficiency' motives dominate until they are satisfied and
only then the 'growth' motives properly emerge. Malsow calls

this process 'self-actualisation' and claims that it opens the way not only, for more profound perspectives on life, but also to, what he calls 'peak experiences'. These peak experiences of awe and mystery can go further and reveal the 'values' inherent in reality. They enable us to see wholeness and perfection (Maslow, 1998).

Although often spiritual in nature, Maslow insists that peak experiences are natural, not supernatural, phenomena. In *Religions, Values and Peak Experiences*, he writes, 'Practically everything that happens in the peak-experiences, naturalistic as they are, could be listed under the headings of religious happenings' (Maslow, 1994:59). He goes on to identify those characteristics, and regards the notion of God as the embodiment of the values that emerge. The spiritual life thus arises from peak-experiences and the individual then develops a private religion of his, or her own. For Maslow, institutional religion is quite separate and secondary.

Creativity

Creativity is another theme in this more positive treatment of personality, and it is implicit in the work of several psychologists of this more humanitarian persuasion, notably Allport, Fromm and Frankl.

Freud takes a negative and pathological view of the creative process and sees a similarity between neurosis and creativity. He felt that both arose from biological drives and from wish fulfilment. Jung is much more positive. In *The Development of Personality*, with reference to those theories which associate creativity with neurosis, he writes:

...the wholeness and healthiness of the creative function is seen in the murky light of neurosis. In this way creativity becomes indistinguishable from morbidity, and the creative individual immediately suspects himself of some kind of illness, while the neurotic has lately begun to believe that his neurosis is an art, or at least a source of art... Disease has never yet fostered creative work; on the contrary, it is the most formidable obstacle to creation (Jung, 1964:115).

However, it is again Maslow who is perhaps the most thorough in his positive examination of this theme. In *Towards a Psychology of Being* he explains that he is less concerned with the 'special talent of the genius type' than with 'the more widespread creativeness which is the universal heritage of every human being'. For him, 'it was obvious that some of the greatest talents of mankind were certainly not psychologically healthy people'. On the other hand, this more widespread creativeness 'seems to co-vary with psychological health' and correlated well with other aspects of the self-actualising individual. He therefore drew the distinction between 'special talent creativeness' and 'self-actualizing creativeness'.

This latter from of creativeness 'sprang much more directly from the personality', and 'showed itself widely in the ordinary affairs of life'. It looked like a 'tendency to do *anything* creatively'. Associated with it was a 'special kind of perceptiveness that is exemplified by the child in the fable who saw that the king had no clothes on'. This kind of creativeness was like the creativeness 'of *all* happy and secure children'. 'It was spontaneous, effortless, innocent, easy, a kind of freedom from stereotypes and clichés' He goes on:

Almost any child can perceive more freely, without *a priori* expectations about what ought to be there, what must be there, or what has always been there. Almost any child can compose a song or a poem or a dance or a painting or a play or a game on the spur of the moment, without planning or previous intent (Maslow, 1998:151-159).

In *The Farther Reaches of Human Nature*, Maslow discusses in more detail the principle characteristics of creativity. It is a long list and only possible to convey something of its flavour in a short paragraph. Creativity is an activity that identifies with the present, and not with the past or the future. It is spontaneous, innocent and devoid of expectations. It is free of the influence of other people. It involves a loss of fear, inhibitions and self-centredness. It involves a gain in strength, courage and independence. It is positive in outlook. It integrates. Research shows there to be a close correlation between these characteristics of the creative person and, what Maslow describes as, the person 'in good psychological health' (Maslow, 1993:59-68).

For Rollo May, in *The Courage to Create*, those who present most directly and immediately the characteristics of the creative person are the artists – the dramatists, the musicians, the painters etc. This is not surprising because he is familiar with the world of the artist and is something of an artist himself. At the same time, he recognises that the creative process represents 'the highest degree of emotional health, as the expression of the normal people in the act of actualizing themselves'. He goes on. 'Creativity must be seen in the work of the scientist as well as in that of the artist, in the thinker as well as in the aesthetician; and one must not rule out the extent to which it is present in captans of modern technology as well as in a mother's normal relationship with her child' (May, 1994:22).

But creativity does not just happen, it requires courage, or the capacity to move ahead despite the difficulties:

Courage is not a virtue or value among other personal values like love or fidelity. It is the foundation that underlies and gives reality to all other virtues and personal values. In human beings courage is necessary to make *being* and *becoming* possible. An assertion of the self, a commitment, is essential if the self is to have any reality. A man or woman becomes fully human only by his or her choices and his or her commitment to them. People attain worth and dignity by the multitude of decisions they make from day to day. These decisions require courage (May, 1994:13-14).

When choosing the title for his book, May had in mind *The Courage To Be*, the book by Paul Tillich, his teacher and friend. In this book Tillich speaks of courage as both an *ethical* and an *ontological* concept. He writes:

Courage as a human act, as a matter of valuation, is an ethical concept. Courage as the universal and essential self-affirmation of one's being is an ontological concept. The courage to be is the ethical act in which man affirms his own being in spite of those elements of his existence which conflict with his essential self-affirmation (Tillich, 2000:3).

Tillich could see little evidence of this courage in the world around him. In writing this book, Tillich was responding to what he perceived as the lack of depth or permanence in the post-war revival of America's religious consciousness. In his Introduction, Peter Gomes quotes from an article by Tillich in the *Saturday Evening Post:*

If we define religion as the state of being grasped by an infinite concern we must say: man in our time has lost such an infinite concern. And the resurgence of religion is nothing but a desperate and mostly futile attempt to regain what has been lost (Tillich, 1958).

That 'infinite concern' was what Tillich understood to be God and which he expressed in a number of ways, most notably as 'the ground of our being'.

For Tillich and May, creativity is of the essence of what it means to be human. Others have expressed similar sentiments. David Wallace-Hadrill, has written in an unpublished autobiography:

> We are most truly ourselves when we are least aware of ourselves in an act of creating. Time and space disappear and we are caught up for a moment into eternity' (Wallace-Hadrill, 1990).

More recently, Karen Armstrong has written:

> We are most creative and sense other possibilities that transcend our ordinary experience when we leave ourselves behind (Armstrong, 2005:313).

Being

On his retirement from Union Theological Seminary in 1955, Paul Tillich preached a sermon entitled, *The New Being* which was later incorporated into a book of the same name. His text for this sermon was from Galations 6:15. 'For neither circumcision counts for anything nor uncircumcision, but a new creation'.

He begins his sermon as follows:

> If I were to sum up the Christian message for our time in two words, I would say with Paul: It is the message of a "New Creation." We have read something of the New Creation in Paul's second letter to the Corinthians. Let me repeat one of his sentences in the words of an exact translation: "If anyone is in union with Christ he is a new being: the old state of things has passed away; there is a new state of things." Christianity is the message of the New Creation, the New Being, the New Reality, which has appeared with the appearance of Jesus who for this reason, is called the Christ. For the Christ, the Messiah, the selected and anointed one is

o</br>

He who brings the new state of things (Tillich, 2005).

For the readers of Paul's letter to Corinthians, this New Being is not about circumcision or uncircumcision. Circumcision is about being a Jew, it is about religious rites associated with Judaism. It can stand for everything associated with religion – Christianity, Judaism, Islam. Uncircumcision is about being pagan, it is about the sacrifices offered by pagans. It can stand for everything associated with secular movements – Fascism, Communism, Secular Humanism. The Christian task is not to compare one religion or movement with another but to point to something distinctively new – Jesus Christ.

We should not be too worried about the Christian religion, about the state of the churches, about membership and doctrines, about institutions and ministers, about sermons and sacraments. This is circumcision; and the lack of it, the secularization which today is spreading all over the world is uncircumcision. Both are nothing, of no importance, if the ultimate question is asked, the question of a New Reality. This question, however, is of infinite importance. We should worry more about it more than anything else between heaven and earth. The New Creation – this is our ultimate concern; this should be our infinite passion – the infinite passion of every human being (Tillich, 2005).

This is heady stuff, for Tillich seems to be suggesting that formal doctrines, structures and institutions whether they be religious or secular count for nothing if they do not signal a New Being. But what is this New Being?

The New Being is not something that simply takes the place of the Old Being. But it is a renewal of the Old which has been corrupted, distorted, split and almost destroyed. But not wholly destroyed. Salvation does not destroy creation; but it transforms the Old Creation into a New one. Therefore we can speak of the New in terms of re-newal: The threefold "re", namely, re-conciliation, re-union, re-surrection (Tillich, 2005).

He then expands on these three 'marks' of renewal which point towards a new state of being which transcends any human constructs and is firmly centered in God, 'the ground of our being', in Tillich's familiar phase. It is beyond the scope of this book to consider these marks of renewal in more detail but the direction in which they point is clear. But what has this to do with authority?

In a later chapter in *The New Being* entitled *"By What Authority?"*, Tillich's text is from Luke 20:1-98:

One day, as he was teaching the people in the temple and preaching the gospel, the chief priests and the scribes with the elders came up and said to him, "Tell us by what authority you do these things, or who it is that gave you this authority." He answered them, "I also will ask you a question; now tell me, Was the baptism of John from heaven or from men?" And they discussed it with one another, saying, "If we say, 'From heaven,' he will say, 'Why did you not believe him?' But if we say, 'From men,' all the people will stone us; for they are convinced that John was a prophet." So they answered that they did not know whence it was. And Jesus said to them, "Neither will I tell you by what authority I do these things."

Tillich continues:

The story we have read was very important to the early Christians who preserved it for us. If we look at it superficially, no reason seems to exist for such a high valuation: the Jewish leaders tried to trap Jesus by a shrewd question, and

Jesus trapped them by an even shrewder question. It is a pleasant anecdote. But is it more than this? Indeed, it is infinitely more. It does something surprising: it answers the fundamental question of prophetic religion by not answering it. An answer to the question of authority is refused by Jesus, but the way in which He refuses the answer *is* the answer (Tillich, 2005).

Tillich's argument is not easy to follow but it has to do with the root meaning of the word 'authority' which is discussed earlier in this book. In his book, *Authority, Leadership and Conflict in the Church*, Paul Avis describes the word 'authority' as:

> ...profoundly liberational and therapeutic. It stems from the Latin verb *augere*, to make increase, to cause to grow, to fertilize, to strengthen or enlarge. This gave the noun root *auctor*, a doer, caser, creator, founder, beginner or leader. The senses of enabling and nurturing are fundamental (Avis, 1992).

However, in common usage, the word does not usually have this positive sense. More often than not it implies something imposed. It is rarely 'liberating' and rarely nurtures 'growth'. It imposes restrictions by reference to law or custom. It is negative and confines or subjugates the aspirations of both individuals and groups. It engenders decrease and decline.

Yet it is possible to see elements of a more positive meaning for authority in the context of our daily lives. And Christians would claim that when authority is understood properly within the Church then indeed it can promote the more positive sense. The authority of scripture, tradition, reason and experience can indeed be 'liberating' and can promote 'growth' if handled carefully.

But, for Tillich, all those authorities which quite rightly

circumscribe our lives both inside and outside the Church are what he calls 'preliminary authorities' and have 'no ultimate significance' even when they are the best they can be.

> The authority of wisdom and authority on earth are not the consecrated image of the authority of heavenly omniscience, but it is the tool through which the Spiritual qualities of humility and knowledge and wisdom are mediated to us. Therefore the wise ones should be honoured but not accepted as unconditional authorities... the social authorities should be accepted as guarantees of external order but not as those which determine the meaning of our lives (Tillich, 2005).

There is an important lesson here for all those who claim 'absolute' authority for any of these 'preliminary authorities'.

The extremes of religious authority

Introduction

In his book, *Authority: A Christian Interpretation of the Psychological Evolution of Authority,* Jack Dominian observes that alongside the decline in some aspects of authority, there is an increase in our understanding of the development of the human personality. He argues that nothing must hinder that growth.

That is not to say that rules and regulations have no place. Of course they have, when they are clearly seen to be no obstacle to the social and emotional interaction that love demands, nor to hinder its growth, which ultimately depends on the continuous development of the personality. The failure of growth of the personality... means that thinking, feeling and action are controlled through fear, anxiety and therefore result in narrow, limited and protective behaviour (Dominian, 1976: 10).

Authoritarianism

In addressing some of the dangers of authority, Dominian draws a distinction between the person who is exercising and obeying authority and the authoritarian personality. For him, the authoritarian personality is,

> ...certainly not someone who is exercising authority, but someone who approaches his own authority and that of others in a particular way and who also tends to have certain other characteristics which together form a distinctive and easily recognisable personality (Dominian, 1976: 11).

He refers to the research undertaken after the Second World War by the American Jewish Committee which led to the publication of *The Authoritarian Personality* (Adorno, Frenkel-Brunswick et al. 1950). The sufferings of the Jewish community under the Nazi occupation were 'clearly a determining influence on such research'. It pointed to 'a combination of features that identified the prejudiced, authoritarian person with the characteristics of the Fascist personality'.

> Such a person is one who, in addition to the tendency to be racially prejudiced and ethnocentric – feels secure when he has his niche within a social hierarchy, who is submissive to those above him and dictatorial to those below him... respectful and subservient towards authority, brusque and rather contemptuous towards his subordinates, repressive of his own instincts, conservative and convention-bound in his beliefs, generally opposed to licence and self-indulgence and in favour of discipline, and punitive and unsympathetic, towards "sinners", particularly if they are judged "inferior" in some way' (Wright, 1971:188; Dominian, 1976: 11).

In the conclusion to their book, the authors note that,

> ...the most crucial result of the present study... is the demonstration of close correspondence in the type of approach and outlook a subject is likely to have in great variety of areas, ranging from the most intimate features of family life and sex adjustment through relationships to other people in general, to religion and to social and political philosophy. Thus a basically hierarchical, authoritarian, exploitative parent-child relationship is apt to carry over into a power-orientated, exploitatively dependent attitude towards one's sex partner and one's God and may well culminate in a political philosophy and social outlook which has no room for anything but a desperate clinging to what appears to be strong and a disdainful rejection of whatever is relegated to the bottom (Adorno, Frenkel-Brunswick et al. 1950: 971)

There is clearly scope for such individuals in any situation where questions of authority and discipline arise, not least in the Church where the use and misuse of power and authority remain live issues. Such issues concern not just the role of the ordained but also of the lay members of the community

Dogmatism

Closely associated with authoritarianism is dogmatism and the research published as *The Open and Closed Mind* (Rokeah, 1960), which has led to the description of the 'open' and 'closed' minds as it relates to the belief system of individuals. The author's suggest 'a basic characteristic that defines the extent to which a person's system is open or closed' as,

> ...the extent to which a person can receive, evaluate, and act on relevant information received from the outside on its own merits, unencumbered by irrelevant factors in the situation arising from within the person of from the outside (Rokeah, 1960:57).

Again, there are many within our churches who have closed minds on biblical, theological or other religious issues, and who are unable or unwilling to consider alternatives to their unchanging and unyielding views. This may be due to both internal and external pressures.

> Examples of irrelevant internal pressures that interfere with the realistic reception of information are unrelated habits, beliefs, and perceptual cues, irrational ego motives, power needs, the need for self-aggrandizement, the need to allay anxiety, and so forth. By irrelevant external pressures we have in mind most particularly the pressures of reward and punishment arising from external authority (Rokeah, 1960:57).

Both the authoritarian and dogmatic personalities are, from Dominian's clinical experience, often the products of anxiety and insecurity.

> Frequently such a man or women is more than averagely anxious. This anxiety leads to insecurity which requires the most powerful and effective protection. This protection is to be found in authority which in turn supplies the basis of certainty and guarantees immunity from all personal weakness and uncertainty. Those in authority are then treated with awe and respect for they become in some way the source of life for the individual who feels at the edge of a personal precipice (Dominian, 1976:14).

In his comprehensive treatment of fear in *Christianity and Fear: A Study in History and in the Psychology and Hygene of Religion*, Oscar Pfister treats fear from a Freudian perspective. He quotes from the familiar biblical passage, 'There is no fear in love, but perfect love casts out fear; for fear has to do with punishment, and whoever fears has not reached perfection in love' (1John 4:18). He describes fear as the 'disturbance of love', and concludes a section on Jesus as follows,

> ...the historical importance of the work of Jesus consisted in the fact that he displaced conscience, a strict authority promoting the formation of fear and of compulsion, in favour of love, a milder and kindly authority. He subordinated the rules of "Thou shalt" and "Thou shalt not" to an absolute power of love... and thereby broke the rule of law with its elements of fear-compulsion-neurosis... (Pfister, 1948: 215).

Blind Obedience

Dangers are also associated with the blind obedience to

authority. In their book, *Crimes of Obedience*, Kelman and Hamilton describe a number of examples of military and other crimes in which defence arguments in court are based on the claim that those who carried out these crimes were merely obeying orders. The Nuremburg trials of 1946 are the most obvious example but other examples of what the authors describe as 'sanctioned massacres' include the My Lai Massacre in Vietnam in1968, and the mass suicide, under the directive of Jim Jones, at Jonestown in 1978. The authors argue that these events cannot be adequately explained by psychological factors, and that social processes which they call authorisation, routinisation and dehumanisation play an important role.

> Through authorisation, the situation becomes so defined that the individual is absolved of the responsibility to make personal moral choices. Through routinisation, the action becomes so organised that there is no opportunity for raising moral questions. Through dehumanisation, the actors' attitudes toward the target and toward themselves become so structured that it is neither necessary nor possible for them to view the relationship in moral terms (Kelman and Hamilton, 1989: 16).

An important study was carried out by Hannah Arendt following the trial and execution of Adolf Eichmann for Nazi war crimes in 1962. In *Eichmann in Jerusalem: A Report on the Banality of Evil*, she argues against the common assumption that such people are always sadists, and claims that they are often very ordinary people just obeying orders. Her views remain controversial.

Stanley Milgram's Experiments
The apparent willingness of adults to go to almost any lengths on the command of an authority is the focus of an important series of experiments carried out by Stanley Milgram in the 1960s. In his

first account of these experiments, *Behavioral Study of Obedience,* in the *Journal of Abnormal and Social Psychology,* published in 1963, Milgram framed his project in the context of the Holocaust.

> Obedience, as a determinant of behaviour, is of particular relevance to our time. It was been reliably established that from 1933-45, millions of innocent persons were systematically slaughtered on command. Gas chambers were built, death camps were guarded, daily quotas of corpses were produced with the same efficiency as the manufacture of appliances. These inhuman policies may have originated in the mind of a single person, but they could only be carried out on a massive scale if a very large number of people obeyed orders (Milgram, 1963:371).

In, *Obedience to Authority: An Experimental View,* he describes, in detail, the series of experiments which he carried out. His objective was to find out the limits of obedience in a situation which involved inflicting pain on another human being. Although no electric shocks were actually administered, those 'teachers' who were the subjects of the experiment thought they were administering increasing levels of shock to 'learners' who progressively failed to give correct answers to their questions. Their response to the demand from the 'instructor' that they should continue to increase the 'voltage' despite cries of pain was monitored. In many cases the 'teacher' obeyed the orders of the 'instructor' to continue to punish the 'learner' in spite of the apparent increasing discomfort of the 'learner'.

In his 1963 publication, Milgram states that,

> Of the 40 subjects, 26 obeyed the orders of the experimenter to the end, proceeding to punish the victim until they reached the most potent shock available on the shock generator. At that point, the experimenter called a halt to the session. (The

maximum shock is labelled at 450 volts, and is two steps beyond the designation: Danger: Severe Shock.) (Milgram, 1963:376).

In addition to the unexpectedly high proportion of obedient subjects, Milgram also found high levels of stress in those participating. One observer commented as follows,

> I observed a mature and initially poised businessman enter the laboratory smiling and confident. Within 20 minutes he was reduced to a twitching, stuttering wreck, who was rapidly approaching a point of nervous collapse. He constantly pulled on his earlobe, and twisted his hands. At one point he pushed his fist into his forehead and muttered: 'Oh God, let's stop it.' And yet he continued to respond to every word of the experimenter, and obeyed to the end (Milgram, 1963:4).

Milgram then embarked on a series of experiments with different 'situational variables', including the proximity of participants, and the conduct of the experiment. The results showed that the situation in which the experiment was carried out was a significant factor.

In 1995, the *Journal of Social Studies* devoted one of its issues to Milgram's experiments under the title, *Perspectives on Obedience to Authority: The Legacy of the Milgram Experiments*. In an introductory article the authors comment that 'many readers have interpreted Milgram's initial obedience repost (1963) as suggesting that people are intrinsically subservient to the dictates of malevolent authority'. They go on,

> However, this was not Milgram's intended message. Rather, the primary conclusion is that most people have a surprisingly broad repertoire of potential responses to social influence. The option actually chosen – to yield or remain independent, to

obey or to defy authority – is often a function of precise situational arrangements rather than intrinsic characterological traits of the person (Miller, Collins et al. 1995:8).

Ethical considerations have meant that it has been difficult to repeat Milgram's experiments. However, an experiment was recently carried out in which researchers used a similar paradigm to the one used by Milgram but within a 'virtual' environment. Although, the researchers did not set out to study obedience, the results did throw light on the issue.

Our experiments show that it is possible to set up a situation in virtual reality where people will comply with requests to follow instructions that appear to cause pain to another entity thus causing discomfort to themselves (Slater, Antley et al. 2006).

The experiment is important, not only because it opens the way for experiments to be carried out in 'virtual' mode that might in 'reality' cause ethical or other difficulties, but also because it extends the range of psychological research.

The Lucifer Effect

Philip Zimbardo is a professor of psychology at Stanford University. In 2007 he published, *The Lucifer Effect: How Good People Turn Evil,* which recalls the Stanford Prison Experiments of 1971 which he conducted at the university and the abuse of prisoners in 2003 at Abu Ghraib prison in Iraq. In Zimbardo's book these two events form a parallel narrative.

The Stanford Prison Experiment was conducted at the university in 1971 by a team of researchers led by Philip Zimbardo. Twenty-four male students were selected to take on randomly assigned roles of prisoners and guards in a mock prison situated in the basement of the Stanford psychology building. The participants adapted to their roles well beyond Zimbardo's expectations, as the guards enforced authoritarian measures and ultimately subjected some of the prisoners to psychological torture. Many of the prisoners passively accepted psychological abuse, and, at the request of the guards, readily harassed other prisoners who attempted to prevent it. The experiment was abruptly stopped after only six days because of the psychological damage that was evidently being done to both prisoners and guards.

The abuses at Abu Graib prison in Baghdad took place during the Iraq War which began in 2003. Personnel of the United States Army and the Central Intelligence Agency allegedly committed a series of human rights violations against detainees. The abuses came to light with reports published in late 2003 by Amnesty International and the Associated Press. The incidents received widespread condemnation both within the United States and abroad, although the soldiers received support from some conservative media within the United States. Philip Zimbardo was an expert witness for one of the Military Police prison guards at the subsequent enquiry.

Throughout the Abu Graib enquiry, Zimbardo was frustrated by the unwillingness of the authorities to consider the possibility that individual failures were not just personal:

> The prosecutor and judge refused to consider any idea that situational forces could influence individual behaviour. Theirs was the standard individualism conception that is shared by most people in our culture. It is the idea that fault was entirely 'dispositional', the consequence of Sergeant Chip Frederick's freely chosen rational decision to engage in evil. Added to my distress was the realization that many of the 'independent' investigative reports clearly laid the blame for the abuses at the feet of senior officers and on their dysfunctional or 'absentee landlord' leadership. These reports, chaired by

generals and former high-ranking government officials, made evident that the military and civilian chain of command had built a 'bad barrel' in which a bunch of good soldiers became transformed into 'bad apples'.

But, for Zimbardo, even consideration of situational factors does not explain the action of these soldiers for there is a deeper malaise – systemic failure:

Had I written this book shortly after the Stanford Prison Experiment, I would have been content to detail the ways in which situational forces are more powerful than we think, or that we acknowledge, in shaping our behaviour in many contexts. However, I would have missed the bigger picture for creating evil out of good – that of the System, the complex of powerful forces that create the Situation. A large body of evidence in social psychology supports the concept that situational power triumphs over individual power in given contexts. However, most psychologists have been insensitive to the deeper sources of power that inhere in the political, economic, religious, historic and cultural matrix that defines situations and gives them legitimate or illegitimate existence. A full understanding of the dynamics of human behaviour requires that we recognize the extent and limits of personal power, situational power and systemic power (Zimbardo, 2007:x).

This last sentence is a salutary reminder that obedience is a function of a range of factors over which individuals do not have full control. This does not absolve them from blame if things go wrong but it does show that issues of obedience are far more complex then we might otherwise have thought. Human beings are vulnerable creatures and despite their best intentions their personal disposition may not be enough to protect them because situational and systemic factors are so strong. There is an important lesson here for the institutional church particularly in relation to the influence of hierarchical structures within the church.

Obedience to legitimate authority is one of the characteristics of the Christian Church, but 'blind obedience' to legitimate authority or obedience to authority exercised illegitimately is clearly a danger. Given the powerful forces at work here and our predisposition to blind and automatic responses, Jack Dominian's warning is prescient.

> For obvious reasons, namely that all response to authority begins in its most elementary, blind and automatic form, we tend to return to that form under stress or uncertainty. It is the most deeply ingrained response and both society and religion have tended to rely heavily on this mode and to turn to this early level when they have been under attack or threat. And yet any hope of really advancing human maturity must depend on encouraging the later levels of personal autonomy which are the very ones that produce the truly personal and human moral response. Traditional morality has always acknowledged the limiting effects of the presence of fear and coercion on free choice and responsibility (Dominian, 1976:42).

Correlations

A large number of correlational studies have been undertaken to establish a link between various measures of religiousness and morality, and surveys of this work appear in several texts (Hood R W, 1996; Wulff, 1997). In general, these studies have shown little correlation between religiousness and humanitarianism, but in respect of some conservative social attitudes correlation has been strong.

The apparent failure of religious involvement to engender

humanitarian behaviour has received its closest assessment in research on conservative social attitudes... Using a variety of measures of piety – religious affiliation, church attendance, doctrinal orthodoxy, rated importance of religion, and so on – researchers have consistently found positive correlations with ethnocentrism, authoritarianism, dogmatism, social distance, rigidity, intolerance of ambiguity, and specific forms of prejudice, especially against Jews and blacks (Wulff, 1997:219).

This statement is too sweeping because both positive and negative correlations have been found and much depends on how these measures of religiousness are defined. In his classic study, *The Nature of Prejudice*, first published in 1954, Gordon Allport writes,

The role of religion is paradoxical. It makes prejudice and it unmakes prejudice. While the creeds of the great religions are universalistic, all stressing brotherhood, the practice of these creeds is frequently divisive and brutal. The sublimity of religious ideals is offset by the horrors of persecution in the name of these same ideals. Some people say the only cure for prejudice is more religion: some say the only cure is to abolish religion (Allport, 1979:444).

In an attempt to understand this paradox, Allport refers to a number of studies and comes to the following conclusion.

Belonging to a church because it is a safe, powerful, superior in-group is likely to be the mark of an authoritarian character and to be linked with prejudice. Belonging to a church because of its basic creed of brotherhood expresses the ideals one sincerely believes in, is associated with tolerance. Thus, the 'institutionialised' religious outlook and the 'interiorised' religious outlook have opposite effects on the personality

(Allport, 1979:452).

In his earlier book, *The Individual and his Religion*, Gordon Allport had discussed what he called the 'mature religious sentiment' which he defined as:

> ...a disposition, built up through experience, to respond favourably, and in certain habitual ways, to conceptual objects and principles that the individual regards as of ultimate importance in his own life, and as having to do with what he regards as permanent or central in the nature of things (Allport, 1950:64).

Although the distinction between 'mature' and 'immature' religion caught the imagination of those working in the field, it was too subjective a notion and too difficult to operationalise.

In their 1967 paper, *Personal Religious Orientation and Prejudice*, Allport and Ross proposed a distinction between an 'intrinsic' and 'extrinsic' religious orientation. Although there are parallels here with the 'interiorised' and 'institutionalised' religious outlook, the distinction now arises not from attitudes to church attendance but from attitudes to religious belief.

> Perhaps the briefest way to characterise the two poles of subjective religion is to say that the extrinsically motivated person *uses* his religion, whereas the intrinsically motivated *lives* his religion... Persons with this (extrinsic) orientation are disposed to use religion for their own ends... (They) may find religion useful in a variety of ways – to provide security and solace, sociability and distraction, status and self-justification. The embraced creed is lightly held or else selectively shaped to fit more primary needs. Persons with this (intrinsic) orientation find their master motive in religion. Other needs, strong as they may be, are regarded as of less ultimate significance,

and they are, so far as possible, brought into harmony with the religious beliefs and prescriptions. Having embraced a creed the individual endeavours to internalise it and follow it fully. It is in this sense that he *lives* his religion (Allport and Ross, 1967:434).

Allport and Ross found that people with an intrinsic religious orientation were less prejudiced than those with an extrinsic orientation. Although, their conceptualisation of intrinsic and extrinsic religion, and their different relationship to prejudice, has dominated research in the psychology of religion for many years, it remains controversial.

In their 1990 article, *Intrinsic-Extrinsic Religious Orientation: The Boon or Bane of Contemporary Psychology of Religion*, Kirkpatrick and Hood raise a number of theoretical and method-ological criticisms of current research, and in his 1997 survey, Wulff concludes that,

> ...the evidence is overwhelmingly against the notion of a single intrinsic-extrinsic dimension; the two dimensions themselves are complex and inadequately defined in opera-tional terms; and what is being pursued may in reality be on the level of general personality variables that are not religion-specific (Wulff, 1997:235)

An alternative conception of ways of being religious is provided by the distinction between 'consensual' and 'committed' religion in the work of Bernard Spilka and his associates (Allen and Spilka, 1967). This distinction has much in common with Allport's original conception of mature and immature religion.

These approaches, however, miss some aspects of Allport's original conception of the mature religious sentiment, and in particular the fact that mature religion involves a readiness to doubt. 'The mature religious sentiment is ordinarily fashioned in the workshop of doubt' (Allport, 1950:73). This led to the introduction of a third dimension by Batson and his associates.

> These characteristics of complexity, doubt, and tentativeness suggest a way of being religious that is very different from either the extrinsic or intrinsic; they suggest an approach that involves honestly facing existential questions in all their complexity, while at the same time resisting clearcut, pat answers… We shall call this open-ended, questioning approach *religion as quest'* (Batson, Schoenrade et al. 1993:166).

As a result of their research they intimate that the quest orientation, not the intrinsic one, constitutes authentic religiousness. Be that as it may, the quest orientation is important for a number of reasons not least of which is that this open, flexible approach, which includes a willingness to doubt, is in direct contrast to the dogmatic approach of fundamentalism.

Fundamentalism

In *The Varieties of Religious Experience*, William James had already recognised this distinction when he implied that it was the dogmatic way in which some religious beliefs are held that may be more closely associated with prejudice,

> And the bigotries are most of them in their turn chargeable to religion's wicked intellectual partner, the spirit of dogmatic dominion, the passion for laying down the law in the form of an absolutely closed-in theoretic system (James, 1982:330).

Although the relationship between fundamentalism and prejudice was extensively explored by researchers, fundamentalism was generally understood to be synonymous with orthodoxy.

This sense of fundamentalism is associated with the movement which began in the late nineteenth century but which became particularly prominent in the period after the First World War. It arose as a reaction against evolutionary theory, liberal theology and biblical criticism. It was expressed in a series of tracts entitled *The Fundamentals* published between 1910 and 1915 supporting five fundamental principles, namely, the verbal inerrancy of Scripture, the Divinity of Jesus Christ, the Virgin Birth, a substitutionary theory of the Atonement, and the physical and bodily return of Christ. It is a movement which has crossed denominational barriers and remains strong within conservative protestant groups, particularly in the U.S.A.

There is, however, another sense in which the word 'fundamentalism' is used. It refers to the way in which beliefs are held rather than the content of those beliefs. In their 1992 paper, *Authoritarianism, Religious Fundamentalism, Quest and Prejudice*, Altemeyer and Hunsberger, drew an important distinction between orthodoxy, and fundamentalism which they defined as,

> ...the belief that there is one set of religious teachings that clearly contains the fundamental, basic, intrinsic, essential, inerrant truth about humanity and deity; that this essential truth is fundamentally opposed by forces of evil which must be vigorously fought; that this truth must be followed today according to the fundamental, unchangeable practices of the past; and that those who believe and follow these fundamental teachings have a special relationship with the deity (Altemeyer and Hunsberger, 1992:118).

Their research showed that there was a positive correlation between fundamentalism and prejudice and a negative correlation between quest and prejudice. In his 1995 paper *Religion and Prejudice: The Role of Religious Fundamentalism, Quest and*

Right-Wing Authoritarianism, Hunsberger summaries these findings as follows,

> ...a religious fundamentalist orientation (and conversely, a non-questing religious orientation), is indeed linked with prejudice and discrimination in the world. There are indications that right-wing authoritarianism is involved in this relationship, with high fundamentalists (and low questors) scoring higher on measures of RWA (Right-Wing Authoritarian) as well as measures of prejudice. Further, it would seem that it is not religious fundamentalism per se that causes prejudice, but it is the tendency for right-wing fundamentalists to be right-wing authoritarians that accounts for the link with prejudice (Hunsberger, 1995:118).

Right-wing authoritarians had been defined by Altemeyer as a combination of three clusters of attitudes,

> Authoritarian submission: a high degree of submission to the authorities, who are perceived to be established and legitimate in the society in which one lives. Authoritarian aggression: a general aggressiveness, directed against various persons that is perceived to be sanctioned by established authorities. Conventionalism: a high degree of adherence to the social conventions that are perceived to be endorsed by society and its established authorities (Altemeyer, 1988:2).

Many of those researching measures of religiousness have constructed scales to assess the strength of the particular aspect that interests them. Since there has been such disagreement about what the core elements of religiousness actually are the number of scales has multiplied. In *Measures of Religiosity*, the authors have gathered together brief reviews of each scale. Their motive is to spread awareness of which scales are already available to the research community and to avoid any duplication and further proliferation (Hill and Hood, 1999).

Humanitarianism

Another perspective on religiousness is provided by Eric Fromm. For him, the difference between, what he calls, 'humanistic' and 'authoritarian' religion represents the most fundamental distinction within the diversity of religious types. 'The essential element in authoritarian religion… is the surrender to a power transcending man. The main virtue… is obedience, its cardinal sin is disobedience… Humanistic religion… is centered round man and his strength'. He goes on,

> Religious experience in this kind of religion is the experience of oneness with the All, based on one's relatedness to the world as it is grasped with thought and with love. Man's aim in humanistic religion is to achieve the greatest strength, not the greatest powerlessness; virtue is self-realization, not obedience. Faith is certainty of conviction based on one's experience of thought and feeling, not assent to propositions on credit of the proposer. The prevailing mood is that of joy, while the prevailing mood in authoritarian religion is that of sorrow and of guilt.

Fromm defines religion as 'any system of thought and action shared by a group which gives the individual a frame of orientation and an object of devotion'. Inasmuch as humanistic religions are theistic, 'God is a symbol of *man's own powers* which he tries to realize in his life, and is not a symbol of force and domination, having *power over man*' (Fromm, 1950:35-38).

Conclusion

It is clear from this brief survey that it is impossible to do justice to the study of authority in the Christian context without some understanding of the psychological factors which govern human behaviour and some appreciation of the situational and systemic pressures that all individuals experience.

Conclusion

'Service is the key to authority'

On the face of it, there is something slightly odd about this statement from Jack Dominian.

In common usage, 'authority' is associated with a 'top down' approach to things. I have already quoted from Richard de George who suggests 'a working model of authority which handles the more obvious cases':

Someone or something is in authority if he (she, or it) stands in relation to someone else as superior stands to inferior with respect to some realm, field, or domain (De George, 1985:14).

There is the sense that one is larger in some way and that the other is smaller. There is the sense that the one is looking down on the other. There is a real sense of hierarchy in our common usage of this word. The headmaster and priest come to mind.

On the other hand, 'service' is associated with a 'bottom up' approach. We think instinctively of the 'service industries' and those who serve us in restaurants and shops. We often treat waiters and shop assistants as 'inferior' people who are there to attend to the needs of the more 'superior' members of society. We expect them to look up to us.

This common usage does not correlate with dictionary definitions of these words because common usage represents a shift in definition and even a corruption of meaning. But common usage does reflect the ways these words are used in popular culture.

This book has been an attempt to show that in the Christian context the way we would wish to use these words is very different from both dictionary definitions and common usage. As Jack Dominian points out 'everyone would agree that service is the hallmark of the use of authority in the New Testament':

> ...whoever wishes to become great among you must be your servant, and whoever wishes to be first among you must be slave to all. For the Son of Man came not to be served but to serve, and to give his life a ransom for many (Mark 10:43-45).

We therefore need to change perceptions but the 'crisis of authority' of the twentieth century which I have already discussed has been exacerbated by the polarisation that is so characteristic of religious discourse in the twenty-first century and any change of perception is going to be hard to achieve.

Polarisation in the debate

On the one hand we see a rise in the number of extreme religious movements within Islam and a consequent spread of international terrorism. These movements claim uncompromising authority within Shariah law to control and oppress anyone and everyone. Some are prepared to go to any lengths including suicide bombing to achieve their objectives. We see a warped sense of the divine and a contempt for the human. Some would say that despite the way in which Islam has been distorted by these movements they represent a reaction to those who seek a reformation in Islam which is long overdue. That may be true but we cannot just sit tight and wait for the moderates within Islam to effect change. It will be some time before the barbarity and of the so called Islamic State can be eliminated. And it is not just in Islam that we see these developments. Hindu nationalism in India has been equally barbaric at times. Tamil separatists in Sri Lanka were the first to use suicide bombs.

Judaism and Christianity also have their extremists. The ultra-orthodox Jews and the extreme right-wing political parties in Israel are uncompromising in their demand for the land which they believe God granted them authority to take for themselves and they are quite prepared to trample on Palestinian aspirations in order to achieve their aims. A two-state solution to this troubled region is quite unacceptable to them. Conservative evangelical Christians and right- wing political parties in the USA are equally uncompromising in their attitude to Islam. Their support for the presidential candidate Donald Trumps's plan to close United States borders to all Muslim immigrants demonstrates the extent of the fear and paranoia that lurks just beneath the surface. Any suggestion that all three Abrahamic faiths might be worshipping the same God is anathema to many people.

On the other hand we see a rejection of traditional forms of Christianity in the western world and a rise in militant atheism. Institutional Christianity is in serious trouble and unless churches can find new ways to express and communicate the faith the decline in attendance is likely to continue. 'Mission' is currently a buzz word within Christian communities but it too often lacks integrity and credibility because its meaning is not clear and because Christians seem unable to drive it forward with any success. People simply do not understand the relevance of the Christian faith in the twenty-first century. Census replies reveal an increasing number of people who positively reject the authority of any religion. The content of the faith and its core beliefs must be reframed if there is to be any progress. People are no longer prepared to sign up to rather abstract propositions.

The rise in 'militant atheism' is relatively new and is largely focussed on the efforts of people like Richard Dawkins and Christopher Hitchins who have achieved considerable notoriety in their diatribe against religion. Their aggressive attacks must be met with a robust defence and their misrepresentation of what people actually believe must be vigorously challenged. The god they deny is not actually a god that many people worship. Their single-minded pursuit of the rational in discourse denies the integrity of other ways of seeing the world. Their commitment to scientific reductionism goes way beyond what other scientists would claim for their discipline. Clashes between science and religion are not new but rarely have the two been so seriously misrepresented. But their cause is losing momentum as people see that there are alternative routes to truth beyond the scientific. Militant atheism takes other forms as for example when any references to religious heritage are forcibly removed from public discourse. Bans on demonstrations of religious allegiance in forms of dress or in the wearing of religious symbols are also becoming enshrined in law.

These two extremes of the authority spectrum are not unrelated for those at one end who hold rigid views of religious authority are motivated in their actions in part by what they see as the rejection of that authority by those whose views are at the other extreme. Similarly those who reject all forms of religious authority are often motivated by the extremes to which other people are prepared to go. And there is tension not just between the extremes but throughout the spectrum of views about these things. In due course tensions will shift and patterns will change but they are unlikely to go away. The reality is that we live in a new world and we have to find ways of dealing with this new crisis. And there would appear to be only one way to go.

Humanity is the key to changing perceptions

We must step outside the conflict and reflect on what unites the different points of view rather than what divides them. And the one thing that unites all those holding such disparate views is the fact that they are all members of the human race. So the way ahead must be to explore what it means to be human. Such a route is likely to be the most productive because it starts from a common base. That may lead some to an understanding of God and others to different conclusions. In my previous book, *A Different Way: A Human Approach to the Divine*, I have argued that Christians can only approach the divine through the human. The

Preface of the book reads as follows:

> This book is based on the premise that we need to encourage more debate in our churches about the essentials of our faith. Such discussion must start with a human rather than a divine perspective. There are two reasons for this. First, it is as human beings that we are embodied as persons, it is as human beings that we engage with the world around us and it is as human beings that we form relationships with the rest of the created order. Second, it as a human being that that which we understand as God was embodied in the form of Jesus of Nazareth, thereby placing humanity at the pinnacle of creation and giving humanity the responsibility for the stewardship of the created (Payne, 2015).

I have also argued that such an approach enlarges our vision of God and enlarges our understanding of what it might mean to respond to that vision. In 1952, the scholar J B Phillips wrote a little book called *Your God is Too Small*. In his Introduction to the book he wrote:

> The trouble with many people today is that they have not found a God big enough for modern needs. While their experience of life has grown in a score of directions, and their mental horizons have been expanded to the point of bewilderment by world events and by scientific discoveries, their ideas of God have remained largely static (Phillips, 1969:7).

Progress will not be made in tackling the 'crisis of authority' until our image of God is worthy of the authority we ascribe to him. Until that time, those who believe in God will continue to have a very limited vision while those who reject God will continue to have no vision at all of a God that they can honour. The way ahead must be to see that our understanding of God is dynamic not static and that we need to mine more vigorously our concept of God for the richness that it contains. Whether we like it or not our concept of God is a human construct whatever the reality beneath so that our different understandings should complement rather alienate each other and enable us to approach that reality more closely. If God is to have authority then he must be much more than the travesty of understanding that we too often hold.

It is appropriate that Jack Dominian should have the last words:

The more each person realizes his potential, the more he achieves autonomy, self-acceptance, inner-directed purpose and meaning, and a love of self which is not a reflection of selfishness or egotism but a plenitude which is available to others in and through love. Such a concept of growth, personal or spiritual, owes nothing to the need to hold on to a 'significant other' for survival, as Freud postulated, but an identification with a significant other called God, who invites us to realize our potential and become like him, not in absolute power and authority, but in absolute love, which is his nature (Dominian, 1972).

Bibliography

Adorno, T. W. (1950). *The Authoritarian Personality*. New York: Harper & Row.

Allen, R. O., & Spilka, B. (1967). Committed and Consensual Religion: A Specification of Religion-Prejudice Relationships. *Journal for the Scientific Study of Religion, 6*, 191–206.

Allport, G. W. (1950). *The Individual and his Religion*. London: Macmillan.

Allport, G. W., & Ross, J. M. (1967). Personal Religious Orientation and Prejudice. *Journal of Personality and Social Psychology, 5*, 432–443.

Allport G. W., (1979). *The Nature of Prejudice*. Cambridge, Mass: Perseus Books.

Altemeyer, B. (1988). *Enemies of Freedom: Understanding Right-Wing Authoritarianism*. San Francisco: Jossey-Bass.

Altemeyer, B, Hunsberger, B. (1992). Authoritarianism, Religious Fundamentalism, Quest, and Prejudice. *The International Journal for the Psychology of Religion, 2*(2), 113–133.

Anglican – Roman Catholic International Commission. (1976). *Authority in the Church*. Anglican – Roman Catholic International Commission.

Anglican – Roman Catholic International Commission. (1981a). *Authority in the Church II*. Anglican – Roman Catholic International Commission.

Anglican – Roman Catholic International Commission. (1981b). *Final Report*. Anglican – Roman Catholic International Commission,

Anglican/Roman Catholic Joint Preparatory Commission. (1968). *The Malta Report*. Anglican/Roman Catholic Joint Preparatory Commission.

Armstrong, K. (2005). *The Spiral Staircase*. London. Harper Perenntial.

Avis, P. (1980). Polarity and Pluriformity in the Church. *King's Theological Review*, 3(2), 55–64.

Avis, P. (1983). The Church's Journey into Truth: A Preface to Further Anglican-Roman Catholic Dialogue. *Theology*.

Avis, P. (1986). *Ecumenical Theology and the Elusiveness of Doctrine*. London: SPCK.

Avis, P. (1992). *Authority, Leadership and Conflict in the Church*. London: Mowbray.

Avis, P. (1997). *Divine Revelation*. Eugene, OR: Wipf and Stock.

Avis, P. (2014). *In Search of Authority: Anglican Theological Method from the Reformation to the Enlightenment*. London. T & T Clark.

Badham, P. (2005). *The Experimental Grounds for Believing in God and a Future Life*. Modern Believing 46 (1)

Baillie, J. (1956). *The Idea of Revelation in Recent Thought*. New York: Columbia University Press.

Baine Harris, R. (1976). *Authority: A Philosophical Analysis*. Alabama: University of Alabama Press.

Batson, C. D., & Schoenrade P. (1993). *Religion and the Individual: A Social-Psychological Perspective*. Oxford: Oxford University Press.

Bereday, G. and J. L. (1961). *Year Book of Education*. London,: Evans Bros.

Borg, M. (2011). *Speaking Christian*. London. SPCK.

Brown, R. E. (1997). *An Introduction to the New Testament*. New York: Doubleday.

Brox, N. (1994). *A History of the Early Church*. London: SCM Press.

Butler, B. C. (1990). The Authority of Love. *The Tablet*.

Chadwick, H. (1967). *The Early Church. The Pelican History of the Church: 1*. London: Penguin Books.

Chadwick, O. (1964). *The Reformation. The Pelican History of the Church*. London: Penguin Books.

Chadwick, O. (1971). *The Victorian Church*. (Part 1). London. SCM Press.

Darwin, B. (1929). *The English Public School*. London. Longmans,

Green & Co.

De George, R. T. (1985). *The Nature and Limits of Authority*. Lawrence, Kansas: University Press of Kansas.

Dominian, J. (1969). The Psychological Roots of Authority. *New Blackfriars, 50*(590).

Dominian, J. (1972). Authority and Paternalism. *The Way, 12*(3), 199.

Dominian, J. (1975). *Cyles of Affirmation:Psychological Essays in Christian Living*. London: Darton, Longman & Todd.

Dominian, J. (1976). *Authority: A Christian Interpretation of the Psychological Evolution of Authority*. London: Darton, Longman and Todd.

Dominian, J. (2006). Letter.

Doyle, T. P. (2003). Roman Catholic Clericalism, Religious Duress and Clergy Sexual Abuse. *Pastoral Psychology, 51*(3).

Edwards, D. L. (1989). *Christian England*. Glasgow: Fount Paperbacks.

Edwards & Wood. (1997). *The History and Register of Aldenham School*. London. Old Aldenhamian Society.

Endean, P. (1993). And it will be for the one being sent: Mission, Obedience and Discernment from Ledochowski to Arrupe. *Centrum Ignatianum Spiritualitatis, 73*, 57–73.

Eno, R. B. (1984). *Teaching Authority in the Early Church*. Wilmington, Delaware: Michael Glazier, Inc.

Evans, G. R. (1992). *Problems of Authority in the Reformation Debates*. Cambridge: Cambridge University Press.

Fisher, P. (Ed.). (2002). *Unpacking the Gift*. London: Church House Publishing.

Fromm, E. (1950). *Psychoanalysis and Religion*. New Haven, Conn: Yale University Press.

Fromm, E. (1994). *Escape From Freedom*. New York. Henry Holt & Co.

Fuller, A.R. (1994). *Psychology & Religion*. London. Littlefield Adams.

Gilkey, L. (1983). God. In P. C. Hodgson & R. H. King (Eds.), *Christian Theology: An Introduction to its Traditions and Tasks*. London: SPCK.

Grant, R. M. (1997). *Irenaeus of Lyons*. London: Routledge.

Guibert, J. de. (1964). *The Jesuits: their spiritual doctrine and practice: a historical study*. Chicago: Institute of Jesuit Sources.

Hardy, A. (1980). *The Spiritual Nature of Man*. Oxford. Clarendon Press.

Harries, R. (1983). *The Authority of Divine Love*. Oxford: Basil Blackwell.

Hill, P. C., & Hood, R. W. (Eds.). (1999). *Measures of Religiosity*. Birmingham, Alabama: Religious Education Press.

Hood, R. W., Spilka, B., Hunsberger, B., & Gorsuch, R. (1996). *The Psychology of Religion: An Empirical Approach*. London: The Guilford Press.

Hunsberger, B. (1995). Religion and Prejudice: The Role of Religious Fundamentalism, Quest, and Right-Wing Authoritarianism. *Journal of Social Issues, 51*(2), 113–129.

Huskinson, L. (2009). *The SPCK Introduction to Nietzsche*. London. SPCK.

Ignatius Loyola. (1996). *Saint Ignatius of Loyola: Personal Writings*. Penguin Books.

James, W. (1914). *Habit*. New York: H Holt & Company.

James, W. (1982). *The Varieties of Religious Experience*. Glasgow: Fount Paperbacks.

Jamison, C. (2006). *Finding Sanctuary*. London Phoenix.

Jesuits. Congregatio Generalis. (1967). *Documents of the thirty-first General Congregation*. Woodstock MD: Woodstock College.

Jung, C.G. (1964). *The Development of Personality*. New York. Pantheon Books.

Kelman, H. C., & Hamilton, V. L. (1989). *Crimes of Obedience: Towards a Social Psychology of Authority and Responsibility*. New York: Yale University Press.

King, E. (1962). *World Perspectives in Education*. London: Methuen

& Co.

Kung, H. (1982). *Structures of the Church*. New York: Crossroad.

Lash, N. (1976). *Voices of Authority*. London: Sheed & Ward.

Lezard, N. (2008). *Worship at the Temple of Folly*. Extracted from http://www.theguardian.com/books/2008/mar/29/featuresreviews.guardianreview29

Macquarrie, J. (1982). Structures for Unity. In M. Santer (Ed.), *Their Lord and Ours*.

McGrath, A.E. (1997). *Christian Theology: An Introduction*. Oxford. Blackwell.

Maslow, A. (1964). *Religions, Values, and Peak Experiences*. Columbus: Ohio State University Press.

Maslow, A. (1968). *Towards a Psychology of Being* (2nd ed.). New York: Van Nostrand Reinhold.

Maslow, A. (1970). *Motivation and Personality* (2nd ed.). New York: Harper & Row.

Maslow, A. (1993). *The Farther Reaches of Human Nature*. New York. Penguin.

May, R. (1994). *The Courage to Create*. New York. Norton & Co.

McConica, J. (1991). *Erasmus*. (K. Thomas, Ed.)*Past Masters*. Oxford: Oxford University Press.

Milgram, S. (1963). Behavioural Studies of Obedience. *Journal of Abnormal and Social Psychology, 67*, 371–378.

Miller, A. G., & Collins, B. E. (1995). Perspectives on Obedience to Authority: The Legacy of the Milgram Experiments. *Journal of Social Issues, 51*(3), 1–19.

Morea, P. (1997). *In Search of Personality*. London: SCM Press.

Murray, R. (1968). Authority and the Spirit in the New Testament. *Authority in a Changing Church*. London. Sheed & Ward.

Nesbitt, P. (2001). *Religion & Social Policy*. Lanham. AltaMira Press.

Niebuhr, H.R. (2006). *The Meaning of Revelation*. Louisville. Westminster John Knox Press.

O'Malley, J. W. (1993). *The First Jesuits*. Cambridge, Mass: Harvard University Press.

Oppenheimer, H. (1974). *The Character of Christian Morality* (2nd ed.). Leighton Buzzard, Beds: The Faith Press.

Otto, R. (1958). *The Idea of the Holy*. Oxford. Oxford University Press.

Payne, R. (2004). *Heirs and Rebels: Aldenham School 1973-1998*. London: Roger Payne.

Payne, R. (2015). *A Different Way*. Winchester: Christian Alternative.

Peters, R. S. (1970). Authority. In A. De Crespigny & A. Wertheimer (Eds.), *Contemporary Political Theory*. New York: Atherton.

Pfister, O. (1948). *Christianity and Fear: A Study in History and in the Psychology and Hygiene of Religion*. London: Allen & Unwin.

Phillips, J.B. (1969). *Your God is Too Small*. London. Epworth Press.

Rafferty, O. (2009). Ahead of His Time. *The Tablet*. 4 May. London

Rahner, K. (1974). Pluralism in Theology and the Unity of the Creed in the Church. In *Theological Investigations* (Vol. 11). London: Darton, Longman & Todd.

Rhode, E. (1968). Films: Life in Britain. *The Listener*. 26 December

Rokeach, M. (1960). *The Open and Closed Mind: Investigations into the Nature of Belief Systems and Personality Systems. American Sociological Review* (Vol. 25). New York: Basic Books. doi:10.2307/2089999.

Sacks, J. (2006). The Torah of Conflict Resolution. *Covenant and Conversation*.

Santos, N. F. (2003). *Slave of All: the Paradox of Authority and Servanthood in the Gospel of Mark*. London: Sheffield Academic Press.

Scott, E. W. (1987). The Authority of Love. In S. Sykes (Ed.), *Authority in the Anglcan Communion*. Toronto: Anglican Book Centre.

Sennett, R. (1980). *Authority*. New York: Random House.

Shaw, G. (1983). *The Cost of Authority: Manipulation and Freedom in the New Testament*. London: SCM Press.

Slater, M., Antley, A., Davison, A., Swapp, D., Guger, C., Barker, C., Sanchez-Vives, M. V. (2006). *A virtual reprise of the Stanley Milgram obedience experiments*. PLoS ONE (Vol. 1). doi:10.1371/journal.pone.0000039.

Society of Jesus. (1996). *The Constitutions of the Society of Jesus and their complementary norms: A complete English translation of the official Latin texts*. Saint Louis: Institute of Jesuit Sources.

Southern, R. W. (1970). *Western Society and the Church in the Middle Ages. The Pelican History of the Church* (Vol. 2). London: Penguin Books.

Stroup, G. (1983). Revelation. In P. C. Hodgson & R. H. King (Eds.), *Christian Theology: An Introduction to its Traditions and Tasks*. London: SPCK.

Stroup, G. (1997). *The Promise of Natural Theology*. Eugene, Oregan: Wipf and Stock.

Sykes, S. (1987). Authority in the Anglican Communion. Toronto: Anglican Book Centre.

Thompson, D. (1995). The Concise Oxford Dictionary of Current English. Oxford: Clarendon Press.

Tillich, P. (1958). The Lost Dimension in Religion. *Saturday Evening Post*. 14 June.

Tillich, P. (2000). *The Courage To Be*. London. Yale University Press.

Tillich, P. (2005). *The New Being*. Nebraska. Bison.

Trotter, W. (1921). *Instincts of the Herd in Peace and War*. London. T. Fisher & Unwin.

Vardy, P. (2003). *What is Truth?* Alresford, Hants. John Hunt Publishing.

Voak, N. (2003). *Richard Hooker and Reformed Theology: A Study of Reason, Will, and Grace*. Oxford: Oxford University Press.

Wallace-Hadrill, D. (1990s). *Final Thoughts*. Unpublished manuscript.

Watt, E. D. (1982). *Authority.* (P. King, Ed.)*International Series in Social and Political Thought.* London: Croom Helm.

Weber, M. (1964). *The Theory of Social and Economic Organisation.* New York: Free Press.

Williams, R. R. (1950). *Authority in the Apostolic Age.* London: SCM Press.

Woodhead, L. (2014). *The Crisis of Religious Authority.* Lancaster University Conference Report.

Wright, D. (1971). *The Psychology of Moral Behaviour.* London: Penguin Books.

Wright, N. T. (2005). *Scripture and the Authority of God.* London: SPCK.

Wulff, D. M. (1997). *Psychology of Religion: Classic and Contemporary.* New York: John Wiley & Sons.

Young, F. M. (1983). *From Nicaea to Chalcedon: A Guide to the Literature and its Background.* London: SCM Press.

Zimbardo, P. (2007). *The Lucifer Effect.* London: Rider Publishing.

Editorial. (1968). Crisis in the Church. *The Tablet.* 3rd August.

Editorial. (2009). What Ireland Now Knows. *The Tablet.* 30th May.

CHRISTIAN
ALTERNATIVE

CHRISTIAN ALTERNATIVE

THE NEW OPEN SPACES

Throughout the two thousand years of Christian tradition there
have been, and still are, groups and individuals that exist in the
margins and upon the edge of faith. But in Christianity's
contrapuntal history it has often been these outcasts and
pioneers that have forged contemporary orthodoxy out of
former radicalism as belief evolves to engage with and
encompass the ever-changing social and scientific realities. Real
faith lies not in the comfortable certainties of the Orthodox, but
somewhere in a half-glimpsed hinterland on the dirt track to
Emmaus, where the Death of God meets the Resurrection,
where the supernatural Christ meets the historical Jesus, and
where the revolution liberates both the oppressed and
the oppressors.

Welcome to Christian Alternative... a space at the edge where
the light shines through.
If you have enjoyed this book, why not tell other readers by
posting a review on your preferred book site.

Recent bestsellers from Christian Alternative are:

Bread Not Stones
The Autobiography of An Eventful Life
Una Kroll
The spiritual autobiography of a truly remarkable woman and a history of the struggle for ordination in the Church of England.
Paperback: 978-1-78279-804-0 ebook: 978-1-78279-805-7

The Quaker Way
A Rediscovery
Rex Ambler
Although fairly well known, Quakerism is not well understood. The purpose of this book is to explain how Quakerism works as a spiritual practice.
Paperback: 978-1-78099-657-8 ebook: 978-1-78099-658-5

Blue Sky God
The Evolution of Science and Christianity
Don MacGregor
Quantum consciousness, morphic fields and blue-sky thinking about God and Jesus the Christ.
Paperback: 978-1-84694-937-1 ebook: 978-1-84694-938-8

Celtic Wheel of the Year
Tess Ward
An original and inspiring selection of prayers combining Christian and Celtic Pagan traditions, and interweaving their calendars into a single pattern of prayer for every morning and night of the year.
Paperback: 978-1-90504-795-6

Christian Atheist
Belonging without Believing
Brian Mountford
Christian Atheists don't believe in God but miss him: especially
the transcendent beauty of his music, language, ethics, and
community.
Paperback: 978-1-84694-439-0 ebook: 978-1-84694-929-6

Compassion Or Apocalypse?
A Comprehensible Guide to the Thoughts of René Girard
James Warren
How René Girard changes the way we think about God and the
Bible, and its relevance for our apocalypse-threatened world.
Paperback: 978-1-78279-073-0 ebook: 978-1-78279-072-3

Diary Of A Gay Priest
The Tightrope Walker
Rev. Dr. Malcolm Johnson
Full of anecdotes and amusing stories, but the Church is still a
dangerous place for a gay priest.
Paperback: 978-1-78279-002-0 ebook: 978-1-78099-999-9

Do You Need God?
Exploring Different Paths to Spirituality Even For Atheists
Rory J.Q. Barnes
An unbiased guide to the building blocks of spiritual belief.
Paperback: 978-1-78279-380-9 ebook: 978-1-78279-379-3

The Gay Gospels
Good News for Lesbian, Gay, Bisexual, and Transgendered
People
Keith Sharpe
This book refutes the idea that the Bible is homophobic and
makes visible the gay lives and validated homoerotic experience
to be found in it.
Paperback: 978-1-84694-548-9 ebook: 978-1-78099-063-7

The Illusion of "Truth"
The Real Jesus Behind the Grand Myth
Thomas Nehrer
Nehrer, uniquely aware of Reality's integrated flow, elucidates
Jesus' penetrating, often mystifying insights – exposing
widespread religious, scholarly and skeptical fallacy.
Paperback: 978-1-78279-548-3 ebook: 978-1-78279-551-3

Do We Need God to be Good?
An Anthropologist Considers the Evidence
C.R. Hallpike
What anthropology shows us about the delusions of New
Atheism and Humanism.
Paperback: 978-1-78535-217-1 ebook: 978-1-78535-218-8

Fingerprints of Fire, Footprints of Peace
A Spiritual Manifesto from a Jesus Perspective
Noel Moules
Christian spirituality with attitude. Fourteen provocative
pictures, from Radical Mystic to Messianic Anarchist, that
explore identity, destiny, values and activism.
Paperback: 978-1-84694-612-7 ebook: 978-1-78099-903-6

Readers of ebooks can buy or view any of these bestsellers by clicking on the live link in the title. Most titles are published in paperback and as an ebook. Paperbacks are available in traditional bookshops. Both print and ebook formats are available online.

Find more titles and sign up to our readers' newsletter at http://www.johnhuntpublishing.com/christianity
Follow us on Facebook at
https://www.facebook.com/ChristianAlternative